Rock'n' Roll

Routledge Popular Music

A series of books for schools edited by
Graham Vulliamy and Edward Lee

Dave Rogers

Routledge & Kegan Paul
London, Boston, Melbourne and Henley

First published in 1982
by Routledge & Kegan Paul Ltd
39 Store Street, London WC1E 7DD,
9 Park Street, Boston, Mass. 02108, USA,
296 Beaconsfield Parade, Middle Park,
Melbourne, 3206, Australia and
Broadway House, Newtown Road,
Henley-on-Thames, Oxon RG9 1EN
Set in 11 on 14pt Helvetica by
Input Typesetting Ltd, London
and printed in Great Britain by
St Edmundsbury Press, Bury St Edmunds, Suffolk

ISBN 0 7100 0938 0

To all the rock'n'roll artists I've not had the space to mention, and, particularly, to Carl Perkins, and to Gene Vincent

I was very lucky. The people were looking
for something different and I came along
just in time

                                Elvis Presley

You know my temperature's risin',
The juke-box's blowin' a fuse,
My heart's beatin' rhythm,
My soul keeps a-singin the blues –
Roll over Beethoven,
Tell Tchaikovsky the news . .

                                Chuck Berry

Contents

Interlude   116
Gene Vincent and Eddie Cochran in Britain 117
Shakin' all over: Johnny Kidd
and the Pirates   120

11 **It doesn't matter any more**   123

12 **Rock'n'roll is here to stay**   127

    Glossary of musical terms   134

    Sources and acknowledgments   139

    **Some suggestions for
    further reading and listening**   144

    Index   147

1 Into the 1950s

I love those dear hearts and gentle people
That live in my home town –
I know those dear hearts and gentle people
Will never ever let me down . . .

Dinah Shore, 1950

Before rock'n'roll, that song seemed to sum up what
pop music was all about. It was certainly tuneful, but
mostly it was sentimental music for adults to feel at
home with. Of course there were children's songs,
like 'Rudolph The Red-Nosed Reindeer' and 'How
Much Is That Doggie In The Window?' But if you
were a teenager leaving school, earning money for
the first time, and wanting to go out and spend it on
enjoying yourself, there was no music which you
could really call your own. The Top Twenty was full
of slow ballads, string orchestras and sing-along
novelty songs like 'Where Will The Dimple Be?' and
'I See The Moon' ('the moon sees me' was the next
line!).

Excitement? There wasn't a lot. In America,
'singing idols' Guy Mitchell and Frankie Laine looked
old enough to be your father. In Britain, Dickie
Valentine and Lita Roza were part of large dance
bands. It was all much too predictable and polished.
There was hardly a guitar in sight.

Johnnie Ray, too, was an early 1950s 'heart-throb', but he was a little different. In 1952 his record 'Cry' topped the charts. Like most of his songs, it was full of emotion – you could hear his voice break with misery. On stage he would fall to his knees and cry real tears. His nicknames were 'Prince of Wails' and 'Cry Guy'! He was tall and thin, and an accident when he was ten had left him half-deaf. But he didn't try to hide his deaf-aid as other stars might have done. It turned out to be an asset for it added to the emotion and his fans loved him all the more.

He was a star right up to the arrival of Elvis Presley. At first the two were compared, for though their music was quite different they did have one thing in common: they both felt what they were singing about. Earlier pop singers, like Perry Como, had been almost polite, crooning songs without showing too much involvement. Ray was the first million-selling pop singer to get inside his songs and put his own emotions on show. The singer was becoming more important than the song, and the image greater than the singer.

It's in every jumpin' honky-tonk wherever you look, It's heard on every corner, and it's even in the Book

In the early 1950s the first music with some guts to catch on in Britain was piano-boogie: music with a bouncing beat and a non-stop rolling rhythm from the left hand playing the bass notes at a fast eight beats to the bar. Tennessee Ernie Ford had a hit with 'Shotgun Boogie', but it was Merrill E. Moore from California whose records sounded best. It wasn't yet rock'n'roll, but it was certainly 'news for dancin' feet'. It was strong, lively and loud, and a long way from the slushy orchestras and cumbersome big bands down at the local dance-hall.

In Britain, Moore's music appealed most to one particular group of young people: 'In '53/'54 his Bell

Bottom Boogie/House Of Blue Lights was a hot
favourite . . . with the first generation of London
Teddy Boys.'

**The Teddy
boys**

Kids came back from evacuation to find their
home surroundings in ruins, especially in London
which was hit worst of all. In many cases their
fathers were still away from home clearing up the
last remnants of the war, and consequently the
kids were able to do almost as they liked. Street
gangs sprang up as a substitute for home life.

Tennessee Teddy

By the 1950s, the clothes the gang-members wore
were an up-dated copy of men's fashion in the reign
of King Edward VII before the First World War.
Originally the new extravagant style was meant for
rich young men-about-town. But, although it was
expensive, the working-class youths of south London
began to wear it and adapt it – tightly fitting trousers
('drainpipes'), fancy waistcoats, and a long, drape
jacket which had sleeves that reached over the
fingertips, and velvet on the turned-back cuffs and
round the back of the collar. At first the newspapers
called them 'Edwardian youths', but soon came the
more popular label, 'Teddy boys'.

Added to the basic suit later came thick crepe-
soled shoes – 'brothel-creepers'. Round the neck,
over a sometimes black shirt, they wore a thin,
straight tie – or a bootlace like one of the black-
jacketed, cheroot-smoking baddies you saw in
cowboy films dealing cards off the bottom of the
pack and shooting anyone who dared call him a
cheat.

And that was the image that went with the style.
Sullen, mean and dangerous-looking, it owed a lot to
westerns and gangster films. It was topped off with

Teddy boy styles
in Newcastle,
1955

the most outlandish hair-styles: long and heavily greased, combed back round each side ending in a DA (meaning 'duck's arse' because that's what it looked like from the back!). At the front it was piled up and back, or fell forward over the forehead in an 'elephant's trunk'. There was even a vogue for Mohican cuts: shaved on both sides leaving a wide strip of crewcut hair from front to back.

The Teddy boys looked at you in a sharp and tense, 'don't-come-too-close' way: 'Don't step on my blue suede shoes,' sang Elvis and Carl Perkins in 1956. They seemed always on edge, but somehow relaxed and unmoved too. Like their American contemporaries who tried to look like film star Marlon Brando, you saw them leaving the dance-hall, the pub or the cinema and 'stopping for a second on the sidewalk as if they were looking for someone

Tottenham, May
1954

who was looking for a fight.' Glancing into a shop window they might put up a hand to check that their hair was still correctly swept back before swaggering off down the street – 'each one of us, in his own mind, a cinema close-up'.

At about the same time came news of a rise in the number of crimes committed by young people. Teddy boys were seen as criminals terrorising their home areas. The newspapers were full of unflattering stories about them, and often reporters' imaginations ran away with them:

> The Daily Sketch exposes the Sunday night gang menace
> THE TEDDY BOYS MAKE THIS A TOWN OF FEAR
> By Owen Summers
> Kingston-upon-Thames, Surrey
> Sunday night
>
> This is a town of fear – fear of the new Teddy Boy gangs. These 'Edwardian' youths, the throw-outs of districts glad to see their backs, swarm in at the weekends. Publicans employ squads of 'strong arm' men, cinema managers seek police protection, local girls keep out of the town on Sunday nights. Police cars are circling round the main streets tonight as I piece together the fantastic story of Teddy Town.
>
> *Daily Sketch*, 3 May 1954

All over the country, cinemas, dance-halls, youth clubs and pubs refused entry to anyone wearing Teddy boy clothes. They were the first large youth group to prompt such a hysterical reaction from society about the way they looked.

The 'affluent society'

So what kind of society was it that produced the Teddy boys and into which rock'n'roll exploded in the mid-1950s?

For young people it wasn't just a question of dressing up. It was a reaction against the suffocating nature of society at the time. The Second World War had ended in 1945, but Britain took a long time to emerge from its shadow. Wartime rationing (which meant that you were allowed to buy only a small, fixed amount of, say, butter or meat per week), had lasted for years. It didn't finally disappear until 1954, the year Bill Haley recorded 'Rock Around The Clock'.

There were still wars of a kind being fought. If you were in the forces there was a good chance of finding yourself on active service in Malaya, Korea, Kenya, Suez or just keeping the peace (though it wasn't very peaceful) in Cyprus. Very likely you'd have been in uniform anyway, even if you weren't sent to any of those places. National Service continued right through the 1950s: like it or not, you had to spend two years in the Army, Navy or Air Force. If you'd left school at fifteen you faced three years at whatever job you could get, knowing that it would come to an end on your eighteenth birthday when your call-up papers arrived in the morning post.

If you were earning money, you quickly realised that hardly anything was produced with you in mind. There were plenty of clothes, for example, for adults and children, but none for you if you were in between the two. The whole idea of being a teenager was a new one. You were still expected to dress like your parents, enjoy the same entertainments, like the same music, even hold the same opinions. It was like getting old before you knew what a good time you could have being young.

But times were changing. Wages were going up. By the mid-1950s the average teenager's weekly *spending money* was over twice the *total* weekly wage he would have received in 1938. Having more money to spend, more things to buy and more leisure-time to enjoy them (the five-day working week was new in the 1950s) was leading to a feeling of affluence. Life was definitely better than it had been in the drab 1940s. More families could afford washing machines, record players and the new tape recorders. Few people owned television sets in 1950, but ten years later it was the centre-piece of most British homes.

As TV-watching grew, cinema audiences dropped. But going to the pictures was still important. There you could forget there was nowhere much else to go and that many towns and cities were still full of bomb-sites. You could escape into the fantasy-world of films. It was the cinema which first became preoccupied with youth – just at the time when young people were starting to be more aware of themselves and becoming more assertive.

But at first it was hard for young people to identify with the film stars – they didn't look young enough. They were too fixed in their attitudes: they couldn't possibly portray the tenseness and uncertain sensitivity of growing up.

Marlon Brando and James Dean changed all that. In *The Wild One* Brando was leader of a motor-bike gang accused of terrorising an American town. By the end he was the local hero, having defeated an even nastier gang of bikers led by Lee Marvin. Wearing leather jacket and jeans, Brando appeared to be playing himself: he *was* the gang-leader, not an actor playing the part. James Dean went one better. In *Rebel Without A Cause* he was a misunderstood

opposite
'What're you rebelling against, Johnny?'
'Whadda ya got?'
– Marlon Brando in *The Wild One*

James Dean,
collar up, hands
in pockets in
*Rebel Without a
Cause*

teenager, outlawed by his fellow-students at high school, and forced to compete in a game of 'chicken' in which his opponent drives off the edge of a cliff and is killed. Dean finally wins respect and understanding through the protection he gives to a weaker classmate.

Brando and Dean were more than just film star heroes. They seemed to have the same fears and enjoy the same things as you. Like the rock'n'roll singers to come, they were young and within reach. When you watched them in the cinema you were them, but, more important, *they* were *you*. Dean died soon afterwards, late on a September afternoon in 1955, when his Porsche sports car collided with another vehicle. He was only twenty-four. He wasn't a rock'n'roll star, but he had the same sort of magnetic appeal. More than Johnnie Ray, but not as much as Elvis to come, James Dean was of the post-war world.

The trouble was, you wanted some action and excitement of your own. Brando and Dean were O.K., but what was missing was the music to go with them: something which helped you give vent to that frustration at having nowhere to go but dance-halls and pubs geared to adults, at feeling independent but not being allowed the freedom – and at having the money but nothing to spend it on. Elvis later sang: 'If you're looking for trouble/You've come to the right place.' The 'right place' was rock'n'roll.

2 Rock around the clock

A 24 year old labourer who kicked in a pane of glass in a greenhouse said in a statement: 'I am sorry I broke it. It's just rock, rock and roll.' He signed the statement 'Teddy Boy', Exeter magistrates were told, but mis-spelt the signature.
Daily Sketch, 25 September 1956

It makes me feel big and great, like I've won a football pool or something.
17-year-old from the Elephant and Castle,
London, September 1956

The week James Dean died, Bill Haley's 'Rock Around The Clock' was entering its fifth month in the American Top Twenty. Two weeks later it arrived for the second time in the British charts, on its way to Number One.

There was no record Hit Parade in Britain before 1952 when the *New Musical Express* started publishing a weekly Top Twelve. But in the United States there was already a weekly list of the top hundred best-selling pop singles, as well as a Country Music Chart, *and* a Rhythm'N'Blues Chart. They reflected the different groups of record-buyers into which the record industry saw the country divided. Local radio stations divided themselves up in the same way too.

Country music by white performers was played by those stations which broadcast to the southern states, where country came from.

Black music – blues and rhythm'n'blues, or 'race music' as the record companies used to call it – was heard on stations aiming at black audiences, not just in the south but in the big west coast and northern cities too, like Los Angeles, Chicago, Detroit and New York.

Before rock'n'roll, record companies in the south were small concerns. They were forced to lend out their most successful recordings to the major companies who could press and sell records faster and in greater quantities. These big companies were always on the lookout for a catchy, saleable song. Their pop singers recorded their own interpretations of country and rhythm'n'blues (r'n'b) hits. Where necessary, they cleaned up the lyrics and smoothed away the rough edges to make them acceptable to listeners unused to country and r'n'b. These cover versions were big hits in the pop chart while the original (and better) singers of the hit songs remained unknown.

'Rock Around The Clock' sold in all three markets. In *Cashbox* magazine it was voted 'No. 1 Record of 1955'. In *Billboard* it was the year's 'Triple Crown Winner', meaning that it had made the most impact on all their charts – r'n'b, country and pop. To add to the confusion, readers of the *jazz* magazine *Downbeat* voted white, ex-country bandleader Haley 'No. 1 Rhythm and Blues Personality of the Year'!

Bill Haley and His Comets   Haley's band played country-boogie and their own versions of r'n'b hits too. They found that young audiences liked these faster, tougher songs best, and Haley changed the band's name from the

Bill Haley complete with kiss-curl, Rudy Pompilli on sax, and the rest of the Comets pose for publicity shots

country-sounding Saddlemen to the Comets, so as to appeal more to a city audience. In New York, in April 1954, they recorded 'Rock Around The Clock'. More than twenty years later Haley talked about those days:

> About this time . . . MGM was doing the movie called 'Blackboard Jungle' . . . and they wanted a song to fit the era of the teenagers, the high school and what have you . . . and so they chose 'Rock Around The Clock' . . . and I think you know the answer from there.

The answer was jiving in the aisles wherever the film was shown. At last a teenage music had begun to arrive. The film told the story of a young teacher at a tough New York school. By trying to understand his often-violent students – and getting beaten up in the process – he finally wins their respect. It was fiction, but to frightened parents reading sensational news stories of 'teenage hoodlums' and 'juvenile delinquents' it seemed very real. To teenagers, however, the film was a breath of fresh air. Here were people their own age doing things they knew something about: at last they could recognise themselves on the screen.

It's got them on their feet again dancing

Bill Haley's song was so successful that he was signed to make a film of his own, telling how he and his band made rock'n'roll popular. It was produced quickly and cheaply, and it wasn't really very good. But that wasn't the point. You weren't going along to see a good film – you went to see Haley and rock'n'roll, and that's what you got. All the big hits were there, and although only on film, in Britain it was the first real rock'n'roll anyone had ever seen. It brought the house, not *down*, but *up* – onto its feet, jiving in the cinemas.

> 'Well, it was this way,' said the diminutive Teddy Boy with the big black dog. 'I'm sitting down near the front, clapping and stamping my feet and singing a bit, when this commissionaire geezer in the blue uniform comes up and shoves his arm across in front of me and shouts: "You're barred." So I grab hold of his arm and pull it and give him a twistie – you know, start the old jive. And then before I know anything, I'm outside.'
> *Picture Post*, 22 September 1956

There was dancing in the streets too: Westminster Bridge was blocked by jiving couples. Newspaper headlines told the story:

ROCK'N'ROLL RIOTS FLARE
ROCK'N'ROLL TERRORISES A CITY
POLICE SQUADS RUSH TO 4 MORE CINEMAS
ROCK'N'ROLL RIOTS FLARE UP AGAIN

Intrigued by all this fuss, the Queen cancelled a special showing of a new Humphrey Bogart film and asked to see *Rock Around The Clock* instead.
Several local councils banned the film altogether:

Five more towns have banned the Rock'n'Roll film 'Rock Around The Clock'. Bradford Fire Services Committee banned it on the ground that 'it contained matter which would be likely to lead to disorder.' Other towns to ban the film are Bristol, where it ran for a week a month ago without any trouble, Liverpool, Warrington and Carlisle.
Daily Sketch, 15 September 1956

It was already banned in parts of London and in Brighton, Birmingham, Blackpool and Belfast. Bury St Edmunds made news by *not* banning it!
In cinemas where it *was* shown, dancing in the aisles was forbidden. In retaliation, seats were slashed open and ripped from their rows. Such incidents were sensationalised in the Press, and – you might have guessed it – Teddy boys were mixed up in it all.

Rhythm-crazed teenagers terrorised a city last night. Police had to radio for help to quell stampedes of Rock'n'Roll Teddy Boys and their girl-friends . . .

13 ROCK'N'ROLL SUMMONSES
13 youths received summonses after the showing of a rock'n'roll film at the weekend.
In one cinema at Dagenham E. (East London) the

film had the crowd ranting and raving, Stratford E.
magistrates were told yesterday. And West Ham E.
magistrates heard how, after 120 youths were
ejected from a Stratford cinema, several were seen
shouting, whistling and jumping over flower beds
opposite the cinema.

Daily Sketch, 4 September 1956

Jumping over flower beds?

To the older generation rock'n'roll came to mean
Teds and violence. The *Daily Sketch* (17 September
1956) reflected this:

'BAN ROCK'N'ROLL FILM SAYS BISHOP'

No wonder parents refused to allow their children to
see the film. If there was still anyone who hadn't
heard of rock'n'roll, the Press gave them a crash
course in its supposed effects.

In Norway and Denmark police used batons to
disperse crowds outside cinemas. There was a riot in
Berlin. Some countries banned rock'n'roll altogether.
And in Singapore 'police were called in to stop British
soldiers jiving in a cinema foyer after a midnight
premiere of *Rock Around The Clock*'.

The Rev. Albert Carter of Nottingham denounced
rock'n'roll from his pulpit: 'The effect of rock'n'roll on
young people is to turn them into devil-worshippers;
to stimulate self-expression through sex; to provoke
lawlessness, impair nervous stability, and destroy the
sanctity of marriage.'

In Miami, Florida, the head of the local censorship
board said she intended to wage a fight against 'this
worm wiggle' via the pulpit and the schools. She
described rock'n'roll dancing as 'nothing more than
shoving boys and girls around' and 'vile gyrations'!

A young American singer turned preacher believed

it led to juvenile delinquency. 'Why I believe that,' he said, 'is because I know how it feels when you sing it. I know what it does to you. And I know the evil feeling that you feel when you sing it. I know the lost position that you get into in the beat.'

Racialist Asa Carter of the North Alabama White Citizens' Council was scared too:

> Rock'n'roll is a means of pulling down the white man to the level of the 'Negro'. It is part of a plot to undermine the morals of the youth of our nation. It is sexualistic, unmoralistic, and the best way to bring people of both races together.

Organisations like hers, along with many other Americans, saw rock'n'roll as inspired not only by the devil but by their political enemy, Communism, as well. However, on the other side of the Iron Curtain they saw it the other way around: Western capitalism was the cause of rock'n'roll.

Many older musicians hated rock'n'roll. British jazzman Steve Race wrote in *Melody Maker*:

> Viewed as a social phenomenon, the current craze for rock'n'roll material is one of the most terrifying things ever to have happened to popular music . . . Musically speaking of course, the whole thing is laughable . . . It is a monstrous threat, both to the moral acceptance and the artistic emancipation of jazz. Let us oppose it to the end.

The end was in sight: right next to his column appeared an ad for Elvis Presley's 'Heartbreak Hotel'!

To unsympathetic listeners rock'n'rollers had 'gimmick voices', sang 'trash', and would have looked better 'if they visited their barbers more frequently'.

One newspaper even foresaw teenagers being
brainwashed (a favourite 1950s' word!):

> It can be used to the most evil purposes by able
> and vicious men. Hitler did it. He would thump his
> chest and say 'Deutschland' three times and a
> hundred thousand audience in Germany would go
> right off on a Nazi rock'n'roll.

But where did rock'n'roll come from? It wasn't just
Bill Haley that all the fuss was about – he wasn't
even a teenager. When he toured Britain in early
1957 his concerts were riotous affairs, audiences
clapping and stamping their feet and – yes – jiving in
the aisles. But when the tour ended so did Haley's
run of success. Like Merrill Moore, he played great,
good-time dancing music. But, as Nik Cohn put it:
'The only trouble was Haley himself. Instead of a
space-age rocker, all arrogant and mean and huge,

'At the Hop' –
Jiving in the
school gym,
Birmingham,
1957

he turned out to be a back-dated vaudeville act.' He
was no Brando or James Dean. Sometimes he
looked as if he didn't quite know what was going on.

Elvis Presley certainly knew. In him, music and
image fused into the man everyone was waiting for.
Rock'n'roll in person. But to understand him we must
go back to the southern country music and r'n'b that
he was listening to as he grew up in Memphis,

Tennessee. Musically this was where rock'n'roll came from, sent rocketing on its way through the loud dance music of Bill Haley and the presence and power of Elvis. For if Haley was everyone's introduction to rock'n'roll, Elvis was chapter one all by himself.

3 Country music

When Elvis was in his teens, country music's biggest-ever star was Hank Williams. All the early white rock'n'rollers said how much they owed him. Hank himself owed a lot to earlier singers, right the way back to the first big country music star, Jimmie Rodgers.

Rodgers was a railroad brakeman from Mississippi and made his first record in 1927. But his career was short: he died of tuberculosis only six years later. Though he was white and sang country music, his songs showed a strong black blues influence. His impact on musicians after him has been so great that he is often called 'the father of country music'.

Country is the music of the white people of the southern states. It began with the settlers of the nineteenth century, travelling west towards the Rocky Mountains. They entertained themselves with folk songs, ballads and hymns from back home in Britain. They turned these into a new style of music for listening and dancing to at hoe-downs and barn-dances to string bands made up of fiddles, banjos, mandolins and guitars. But it remained unheard outside the south. Even when record-making arrived the new record companies in the northern cities ignored it. They didn't know the back-country hills and plains of the south, and they saw no future in this raw, unsophisticated music.

However, with the arrival of radio in the 1920s, record sales dropped. Alarmed, the companies looked around for new markets and sent their recording men into Tennessee and Mississippi. Their cars piled high with microphones and cumbersome disc-cutting equipment (there were no tape recorders then), they set out to find some of this rough music.

Soon radio station WSM in Nashville, Tennessee, started a Saturday-night country show. One night, in answer to a hostile comment from the presenter of the classical music show which preceded it, producer George Hay said: 'For the past hour we have been listening to music taken largely from grand opera, but from now on we will present the Grand Ole Opry.' The show became the Mecca of all aspiring young country players.

Western swing and Bluegrass

You can change the name of an old song,
Rearrange it and make it swing . . .

Bob Wills

After Jimmie Rodgers's death country began to change from the old string band 'hillbilly' style. Musicians in the south-west felt other influences: New Orleans jazz, blues, Louisiana's cajun music and Mexican songs from over the border. Bands added saxophones, trumpets, clarinets, and a piano and an amplified steel guitar. They played music which mixed blues and jazz as well as hillbilly. It was known as 'western swing'. There were many bands as good, but it's Bob Wills who is most associated with it.

Western Swing's natural habitat was the dancehall and a typical Saturday night scene would be a small town-hall in Oklahoma with over 1000 people jammed in, some of whom had driven maybe 150 miles. Most of Bob Wills' fans were working class, just coming out of the Depression, and the worst kind of rural isolation (Milton Brown often played where food was the price of admission, to be given away to the needy after the show) . . . The music was incessant, Wills hollerin' and joking through all the numbers – even ballads – and the old wooden floors would bounce under the stomping feet of foxtrotting dancers.

Drums were included too. Turning its back, the Grand Ole Opry encouraged the old-time string bands. But other changes were taking place too. By the late 1940s the leading band was Bill Monroe's Bluegrass Boys. They came from Kentucky where the grass is so lush it looks almost blue: the Bluegrass State. Monroe's voice was high and 'lonesome'-sounding. He once talked about how he came to sing that way:

I've always liked the touch of blues, you know, and I put some of that into my singing. I like to sing the way it touches me, it makes me feel good. And I like to sing from the heart, and in singing that way I hope it will touch the man that's listening to me, that he will get the meaning of what I'm doing, and it will touch his heart too.

It was Monroe's best-known song 'Blue Moon Of Kentucky' that Elvis recorded in 1954 as one side of his first single.

Honky-Tonk

Well, I went to a dance and I wore out my shoes,
Woke up this morning wishin' I could lose
Them jumpin' honky tonk blues . . .

Hank Williams

Meanwhile the tougher rhythms of honky-tonk were paving the way for rockabilly and rock'n'roll. In bars in roadside shacks (juke-joints or honky-tonks) small groups, black and white, competed with the new jukeboxes.

Since it was so noisy inside, two things happened: customers complained they couldn't hear the jukebox, and the musicians had difficulty making themselves heard above the din. So they added drums to their music and electric amplification to their guitars. They started using a heavier beat too – slapping the strings of the double bass and hitting the guitar to make a chunky, resounding chord: 'sock rhythm' it was called.

> When you step up to a jukebox and you slip a
>   nickel in,
> You can bet your bottom dollar when that record
>   starts to spin,
> You'll hear a fiddle and a guitar with that honky-
>   tonkin' sound,
> It's that hillbilly breakdown that's spreading all
>   around.

Country music was by now beginning to earn big money for pop singers like Bing Crosby. They adapted country songs into a more popular style. In 1950 Patti Page sold a million with her pop cover version of 'Tennessee Waltz' and the record industry finally cottoned on to country as big business. Hank Williams set the seal on its national success.

Hank Williams He came from Alabama where, he said, 'I learned to play the git-tar from an old colored man in the streets of Montgomery.' Hank mostly wrote his own songs. In 1946 when he was twenty-three he travelled to

Nashville to see song publisher Wesley Rose. Rose
remembers that day:

A tall, skinny kid came in with a blond-haired
woman. They looked like average country folks.
The woman said, 'My husband would like to sing
you some songs.' It isn't normally done that way. I
mean, you don't just walk in cold and say, 'Let me
sing you a song.' My father turned to me and said,
'Have we got time?' I said, 'Sure, why not.' It's
lucky we had nothing more important to do than
go to lunch.

The songs Hank went on to record didn't appeal
just to the south; they made the national pop charts
too. His melodies were easy to remember and his
words expressed very simply what he wanted to say.

The woman on our party line's a nosy thing,
She picks up the receiver when she knows it's my
    ring –
Why don't you mind your own business?

He wrote some songs travelling between shows and
described what he saw as the car sped across the
countryside.

The silence of a falling star
Lights up a purple sky,
And as I wonder where you are
I'm so lonesome I could cry.

Most of all he really felt what he was singing. He
once had this to say:

It can be explained in just one word: sincerity.
When a hillbilly singer sings a crazy song, he feels
crazy. When he sings 'I Laid My Mother Away', he
sees her a-laying right there in the coffin. He sings

more sincere than most entertainers because the hillbilly was raised rougher than most entertainers. You got to know a lot about hard work. You got to have smelt a lot of mule manure before you can sing like a hillbilly. The people who has been raised something like the way the hillbilly has knows what he is singing about and appreciates it . . . what he is singing is the hopes and prayers and dreams of what some call the common people.

But the strain of being a star was too much. He became an alcoholic. In 1952 his wife divorced him and he was fired from the Grand Ole Opry. By now his body was damaged from too much drink, too many pills (both to help him perform and to let him relax afterwards), and the stress of a life on the road.

He died a few hours into New Year's Day 1953, alone in the back of a car driving through a snowstorm to a concert in Ohio. They'd reached West Virginia before the driver looked in the back, touched Hank's cold hands and realised he was dead.

Celebrating his eighteenth birthday that same week in Memphis was Elvis, in his last year at school. Eighty miles north-east in Jackson, Carl Perkins, nearly twenty-one and married a year, was singing with his two brothers in local honky-tonks and 'dodging beer-bottles. First when they started fighting we'd play extra loud, then we'd start running out through the windows. Rough, man, rough. I saw a lot of blood in those days.' Further south in Ferriday, Louisiana, Jerry Lee Lewis, at eighteen, was getting ready for his second marriage and also playing in clubs and bars. And over to the west in Lubbock, Texas, later that spring sixteen-year-old

Buddy Holly sat in school and wrote in an English essay: 'I have thought about making a career out of western music if I am good enough but I will just have to wait to see how that turns out.'

But country wasn't all they heard. For the brashness and confidence to match their adolescent mood, Presley, Perkins, Lewis and Holly tuned in their radios to the local black stations. The music they heard there was rhythm'n'blues.

4 Rhythm'n'blues

I'd always enjoyed r'n'b – it was just something we grew up with in Tennessee.

Scotty Moore, Elvis's guitarist

In Memphis, Tennessee, in 1948, radio station WDIA opened up, billing itself as 'America's only 50,000 watt Negro radio station', broadcasting twenty hours a day, seven days a week. Elvis wasn't the only one listening in. Their parents would have been horrified if they had known but lots of other white American teenagers were listening too. Like their contemporaries in Britain, they were fed up with the unexciting pop their parents and elder brothers and sisters were buying. But, unlike the London Teddy boys, American teenagers could flip the dial on their wireless sets and find music that had much more roughness and fire to it.

Radio and jukeboxes had changed black music too. City blacks demanded a more aggressive (and often more sophisticated) music. The old acoustic blues of the south seemed pessimistic and out-of-date. More forceful instruments, the electric guitar and the saxophone, entered r'n'b. Even the singing style changed to express a more confident and self-reliant approach to life. Such changes are discussed more fully in Graham Vulliamy's *Jazz and Blues*.

In the 1930s and 1940s many black people moved from the poor southern states to find work in the industrial cities of the north and west. They took their music with them and it became tougher and harsher. In Chicago records made by the new Chess company still kept links with southern blues but the musicians were electrifying their instruments and playing at near-maximum volume. The music was a pushier, down-town big-city blues: the earlier sock rhythm gave way to Chicago's heavy backbeat, emphasising the second and fourth beats of every bar.

R'n'b bands were formed – their successful years were the 1940s and early 1950s. Rock'n'roll's biggest debt to them was the saxophone. Bandleader Johnny Otis once explained:

> See, that's one thing that made rhythm and blues different from the old-fashioned blues . . . The singer is singing and, instead of just guitars twanging, the horns played whole notes, rolling those riffs near the ends of the choruses – you know, whole notes with little melodies attached to them.

Some white rock'n'roll bands later tried to copy the exciting showmanship of star saxophonists like Big Jay McNeely: 'He fell first on his knees, never releasing the horn, and walked that way across the stage . . . And then he fell backwards, flat on his back, with both feet stuck up high in the air.' Bill Haley's bass-player would spin his double-bass around and play it on his back while the others tried, in vain mostly, to imitate McNeely's antics.

There were singers too along with the screaming saxes. 'Boss of the Blues' Joe Turner was the man who first recorded Bill Haley's 1955 hit 'Shake Rattle

Joe Turner

And Roll'. And, in New Orleans, Roy Brown found success with a more emotional, less-shouted, style of singing. In 1948 he recorded his own song: 'Have you heard the news?/ There's good rockin' tonight . . .' Six years later it was to be one side of Elvis's second single.

However, in the 1940s Louis Jordan's band was the most well known. His music was boogie-based but used saxophones too – jump-band style. His hits – like 'Choo Choo Ch-Boogie', and the tale of the party that went wrong, 'Saturday Night Fish Fry' – anticipated the 1950s by appealing to both black *and* white audiences.

Alan Freed

In the winter of 1951, a record-shop owner in Cleveland, Ohio, noticed that more and more young people, white as well as black, were buying r'n'b records. Intrigued, he mentioned it to local disc-jockey Alan Freed. Freed began playing these records and the listener response was immediate and enormous. Soon his Moondog Show was given over almost entirely to uptempo black music from the r'n'b charts. Freed liked the music too, especially the new, young r'n'b vocal groups from the northern cities – such as the Dominoes, the Clovers and the Drifters. White radio it may have been, but there were few holds barred here.

> There'll be fifteen minutes of kissin',
> Then you'll holler 'Please don't stop!'
> There'll be fifteen minutes of teasin'
> And fifteen minutes of squeezin'
> And fifteen minutes of blowin' my top.
> So if your man ain't treatin' you right,
> Come up and see your Dan –
> I rock 'em, roll 'em all night long,
> I'm a sixty-minute man.   The Dominoes

PC.8383-PB

Alan Freed with
Little Richard and
Bill Haley

Freed was one of the first to programme black music to a white audience. He and Sam Phillips of Sun Records in Memphis were the two men behind the scenes who gave rock'n'roll its first and most important boost.

Rock'n'roll? Yes – for Freed claimed to have invented the name. He was later called a 'nigger-lover' for championing black music, for the name 'rhythm'n'blues' still had 'race'-music overtones. He took the two common terms for sexual intercourse from blues and r'n'b and fused them together to describe this new, forceful, danceable city music. By the time he moved to New York in 1954 and changed the name of his show to Rock'n'Roll Party his faith in the new music was more than justified. For two years he'd been organising r'n'b concerts, first in Cleveland and later at the Paramount Theatre in New York. That first Moondog Ball in Cleveland was cancelled: there was no way to deal with the demand. Thirty-thousand young people, black and white ('a checkerboard audience', one performer called it) turned up for only 10,000 seats. Said Freed afterwards, 'Everybody had such a grand time breaking into the arena . . . that they didn't ask for their money back!'

The segregationists, who were trying to keep the races apart, were horrified. Aghast at the music's roughness and the sexual explicitness of the lyrics, 'decent-living' white middle-class parents were terrified at the effect on their sons and daughters. For a large section of white youth, racial musical barriers were either breaking down or else had never existed. But though Bill Haley's hits plainly borrowed from r'n'b there was still no original, white rock'n'roll. The spark to jump the gap between white and black music was still missing. It was to come from Memphis.

Sam Phillips   It seemed to me that the 'Negroes' were the only ones who had any freshness left in their music; and there was no place in the South they could go to record. The nearest place where they made so-called 'race' records – which was soon to be called 'rhythm and blues' – was Chicago, and most of them didn't have the money or the time to make the trip to Chicago.

Sam Phillips

So in 1950 Phillips opened a tiny recording studio, lending out his tapes to record companies, Chess amongst them. Memphis was within reach of a large area of the south and he didn't have to look far for people to record. Memphis blues was harsh and aggressive – and it existed alongside white country music. Some musicians were beginning to mix the two together and Phillips urged them to sing and play in a rougher manner similar to what was later to become rock'n'roll. His first hit, Jackie Brenston's 'Rocket 88', had the controls turned up high and a distorted guitar sound. Phillips later said this was where he 'started pulling these things – blues, country and pop – together.'

Soon Sam opened Sun Records, producing, promoting and distributing his own records. In 1953 he recorded Junior Parker singing 'Love My Baby'. A heavily amplified guitar rings out over the backbeat of the drums, fighting for prominence with Parker's vocal. The singing was still blues, but the overall sound was approaching rock'n'roll. 'Gimme something different, something unique,' Sam had told Harmonica Frank a few years earlier. Frank was white, in his forties, and had been playing and singing ever since he could remember. His 'Rockin' Chair Daddy' is a great record which almost defies labelling, but, like 'Love My Baby', it was on the way to that 'something unique': a fusion of country and r'n'b – rockabilly, white southern music, the basis of 1950s' rock'n'roll.

But Sam needed an original interpreter who would appeal to the national market – and who had the flash, arrogance and rebellious power of Marlon Brando and James Dean.

Late in 1953, eighteen-year-old Elvis Presley, not long out of school, came into the Sun office to make a record as a present for his mother. That afternoon, Phillips's office manager Marion Keisker kept a tape of what Elvis had cut.

> Over and over I remember Sam saying 'If I could find a white man who had the Negro sound and the Negro feel, I could make a billion dollars.' This is what I heard in Elvis, this . . . what I guess they now call 'soul' this Negro sound. So I taped it. I wanted Sam to know.

Sam was interested, but it was another few months before Elvis entered the studio again. In the meantime it was more than just his singing that had intrigued Marion: 'Funny thing is I came home and was telling about him and my mother said, "Oh, I've seen that kid on the streetcar. The kid with the sideburns." Those days, nobody had sideburns.'

5 Good rockin' tonight

'I heard the news', Elvis would sing in 'Good Rockin' Tonight' – but he was the news.

Greil Marcus

Soon Sam Phillips found a song he thought might sell, but he needed someone to record it. Marion reminded him of 'the kid with the sideburns' and picked up the phone to dial the number Elvis had left. 'I was still standing there with the telephone in my hand and here comes Elvis, panting. I think he ran all the way.'

(Elvis Aaron Presley was born in Tupelo, Mississippi, on 8 January 1935. His father was a farmworker. Elvis was devoted to his parents, especially his mother, who died in 1958 and for whom he'd made that first private recording. When he was thirteen, the family moved to Memphis, his father to a job packing cans at a paint factory, and Elvis to Humes High School.)

The song and Elvis didn't fit. But Phillips rounded up two members of a hillbilly band he'd recorded before and started them rehearsing with Elvis to see if anything should come of it. They were guitarist Scotty Moore and double-bass player Bill Black. At first they weren't too keen but after a lot of work in

the studio, and a good deal of urging from Phillips to
'Keep it simple, keep it simple', they decided to put
something down on tape.

('It was a lower poverty-type school, one of the
lowest in Memphis. I wouldn't have taken much for
that school and I don't think Elvis would've either
. . . In that neighbourhood the fact that Elvis got
through without getting into serious trouble was an
accomplishment.' Buzzie Forbess, schoolfriend of
Elvis.)

July 1954   It's late and in the tiny, stuffy studio on
Union Street the recording hasn't been going too
well. Elvis, Scotty and Bill are working well together,
but neither they nor Sam at the controls are really
satisfied: they all sense that the 'something unique'
hasn't happened yet.

They take a break, drinking and chatting, and the
talk turns to blues. Elvis mentions Arthur Crudup, a
blues singer he particularly admires. He strums his
guitar, begins to sing one of Crudup's songs 'That's
All Right Mama', and Scotty and Bill pick up the
rhythm behind him, Bill slapping his bass strings
hard, Scotty adding little melodic fills on lead. 'Just
making a bunch of racket, we thought,' remembers
Scotty. 'The door to the control room was open, and
when we was halfway through the thing, Sam came
running out and said "What in the devil are you
doing?" We said, "We don't know". He said, "Well,
find out real quick and don't lose it. Run through it
again and let's put it on tape." '

It was to be the top side of Elvis's first single. A
few nights later they had the B-side too: Bill
Monroe's old Bluegrass song 'Blue Moon Of
Kentucky'. As they record the song, Elvis reaches
deep down into it, his voice alternately high country

and committed blues. Scotty and Bill follow him, lose touch, try again, and storm to a finish that leaves the guitar still strumming, winding down as they become almost embarrassed at their depth of concentration.

Now, here was that 'something unique' and they all knew it. '*Damn*, nigger!' says Scotty to Elvis, who laughs shyly. 'Fine, fine, man,' says Phillips, 'Hell, that's different! That's a *pop song* now, Levi! That's good!'

Excitedly they listen to the finished playbacks of the two songs. 'Good God, they'll run us outa town when they hear it!' exclaims Sam. For in that first record the fusion is made. One side is blues with Scotty and Bill playing almost country – the other, hillbilly but Elvis's voice making blues music.

> ('They weren't noisy parties; nothing like that. Instead of records Elvis would play and sing, but it wasn't noisy. Elvis was always doing that at parties and so we learned to dance before he did. We were conforming to the dances of the time . . . Elvis had his own movements of course, and eventually we all came around to his way. I remember seeing him in front of a jukebox one time, listening to the record and imitating playing a guitar and doing these moves.' – Buzzie Forbess, schoolfriend of Elvis)

Sam Phillips remembers how that first record confused – and angered – disc-jockeys. 'I recall one jockey telling me that Elvis Presley was so country he shouldn't be played after five a.m. and others said he was too black for them.' When Elvis began playing local shows audiences were divided. Some were just polite, some hated him. But others, young people mostly, went crazy over precisely what made the others hate him most: the sexy movements, his wild clothes (he was wearing pink slacks and shirt even when Scotty first met him), that brooding handsome face – and those sideburns. But it was the music too, and the inescapable fact that this was no act: music and image fused, the one was part of the other.

('You'd see this frenzied reaction, particularly from the young girls. We hadn't gone out and arranged for anybody to squeal and scream. Not like Frank Sinatra did in the forties. These girls screamed spontaneously . . . For Elvis they just did it automatically.' – Bob Neal, Elvis's first manager)

The Grand Ole Opry didn't like him, but other shows did. And when they saw him everyone was surprised that just three people could produce the full, echoed sound that came off the record. Turning up the volume, urging roughness and simplicity, adding echo to music which, coming from that tiny studio, could have sounded so cramped – all Phillips's searching and experiments and ideas of the past four years turned Elvis, Scotty and Bill's music into a sound you couldn't ignore. This was nobody's background music. It leapt out of the radio and jukebox, killing idle conversation and demanding response, to listen, to dance, just to move with it.

('Plus, it was almost frightening, the reaction that came to Elvis from the teenaged boys. So many of them, through some sort of jealousy, would practically hate him. There were occasions in some towns in Texas when we'd have to be sure to have a police guard because somebody'd always try to take a crack at him. They'd get a gang and try to waylay him or something. Of course, Elvis wasn't afraid of them and was quite willing to defend himself – and did on occasion.' – Bob Neal)

And what was the music they'd made? It was the mixture of country and blues that was rockabilly. Acoustic music – amplified, yes – but with the rhythm emphasised by the hard-slapped strings of a big double bass. Drums would be added later when D. J. Fontana joined them. 'Cat music' was what r'n'b was called in Texas, and Elvis was billed on some shows as 'The Hillbilly Cat'. To others he was 'The King of Western Bop'. Confusion was in the air, but one thing was certain: with Phillips at the controls, Elvis, Scotty and Bill had crossed musical and racial barriers and come up with the first true white rock'n'roll – rockabilly.

('This cat came out in red pants and a green coat and a pink shirt and socks, and he had this sneer on his face and he stood behind the mike for five minutes, I'll bet, before he made a move. Then he hit his guitar a lick, and he broke two strings. I'd been playing ten years, and I hadn't broken a *total* of two strings. So there he was, these two strings dangling, and he hadn't done anything yet, and these high school girls were screaming and fainting and running up to the stage, and then he started to move his hips real slow like he had a thing for his guitar . . . He made chills run up my back, man, like when your hair starts grabbing at your collar.' – rockabilly and country singer Bob Luman)

Inspired, all over the south, white singers followed suit. Eddie Cochran and Buddy Holly watched his shows and changed their styles accordingly. Jerry Lee Lewis sat up and took notice. Johnny Burnette, at the same school as Elvis, recorded some even wilder rockabilly. Carl Perkins knew this was the music he'd been working towards too, and finally persuaded Sam Phillips to agree with him.

By the autumn of 1955, Elvis had a new manager, Colonel Tom Parker, a long-time showman and country music entrepreneur who'd also been involved in travelling medicine shows and county fairs. Mention any of that type of business to him and he'd tell you he'd done it. Parker remained his manager until Elvis's death in 1977. He was flamboyant, forceful, and, as controller of Elvis's affairs, extremely astute. Stories about him abound. Once he dipped sparrows in yellow paint and sold them as canaries. Another time he sold photos of Elvis outside one of his shows, and then after the performance searched the theatre for dropped photos to sell again in the next town.

The Colonel became more and more involved. At last, in November 1955, he went to New York to negotiate a record deal with whichever of the big national companies came up with the best offer. In Nashville, Elvis had just been voted the most promising new country artist and his latest record was at the top of the country charts. It was Junior Parker's old song 'Mystery Train'. Elvis's voice is full of arrogant self-confidence, completely assured, and Scotty Moore's playing borrows directly from the solo on 'Love My Baby' the other side of Parker's original record of two years earlier.

On 17 November the Colonel clinched a deal with RCA-Victor. For the then-huge sum (for a national unknown) of $40,000 RCA bought Elvis from the tiny Sun Records of Memphis. RCA knew they had a good commercial proposition in this country boy with the weird name. They were going to promote him in all three markets: pop, country and r'n'b. But as Elvis entered their studios in Nashville for the first time, in January 1956, they could not have guessed that they had the real explosion of rock'n'roll worldwide under contract.

Roll over Beethoven, and Bill Haley too. It was 1956 and rockabilly and rock'n'roll were about to go global.

6 Hail, hail, rock'n'roll: America in the mid-1950s

All my friends are boppin' the blues –
I must be rhythm-bound.

Carl Perkins

Tuesday 10 January 1956 RCA's studio, Nashville, Tennessee. Elvis is recording for the first time away from Sam Phillips and Memphis. Scotty, Bill and drummer D. J. Fontana are there, but RCA has added its own sessionmen. The song is 'Heartbreak Hotel', and when the session is over, Elvis and the band go back on the road, a gruelling one-nighter tour to complete.
Saturday 28 January The Dorsey Brothers TV show.

In living rooms all over the country the small-screen television sets went dark for a second and when the picture returned, Elvis was standing center-stage, gazing into the camera with his dark lidded eyes. He moved his shoulders slightly, adjusting the draped sport jacket he was wearing, relaxed his wide-spread legs, snapping his right leg almost imperceptibly. 'Wellllll, since mah beh-bee left me/ Ah've found a new place to dwell/ It's down at the end of Lonely Street/ It's Heartbreak Hotel . . .' As Scotty came in on guitar, Elvis's legs jerked and twisted. He thumped his own guitar on the afterbeat, using it as a prop and almost never playing it now. He bumped his hips. He moved his legs in something that seemed a cross between a fast shuffle and a Charleston step. He sneered, dropped his eyelids and smiled out of the left side of his mouth. He used every physical trick that had come to him in the sixteen months since his first record was released, tricks which were polished by repeated use, but still natural and spontaneous. The television audience had never seen anything like it . . . Elvis Presley was 'doing it'. On television. Coast to coast.

Friday 4 February   'Heartbreak Hotel' is released. The secret is out. The 'race' music you weren't supposed to know about, the wild gyrations (Elvis the Pelvis) of the black performers Elvis had watched, were right out in the open at last: on national TV, in the newspapers, and on the record players of a generation of white teenagers.

The record shot up the country, r'n'b *and* pop charts. Sam Phillips was right. To the horror of the older generation, Presley was a pop singer now and there was no stopping his success. Confused, adult white America struggled to cope with it.

> You ain't nuthin' but a hound dog,
> Cryin' all the time . . .

Ed Sullivan declared he would never allow Elvis on his prestigious TV show. Within a few weeks he was offering him $50,000. But he gave the cameramen orders to show Elvis only from the waist up, so as not to offend his adult audience – and to protect younger viewers!

> They said you was high-class,
> Well, that was just a lie . . .

opposite
Elvis on stage with the Jordanaires, the backing group supplied by RCA

A British magazine ran a competition, first prize to go
to the sender of the correct lyrics of 'Hound Dog'. A
put-up job. In the end they announced there was no
winner: not even their 'experts', they said, could
decipher the words!

Elvis seemed to take in all the frustrations of his
teenage audience and explode back at them, forcing
them to define their own image, create their own
space, take possession of their own world. The
exhilaration that he felt can be heard in all his
records of the time – it jumps out at you,
transforming even the weakest song into 'something
unique'. It was as if he had become rock'n'roll in
person and burst open the door of the adult
establishment.

Colonel Parker was soon able to claim: 'When I
first knew Elvis, he had a million dollars worth of
talent. Now he has a million dollars.'

The music meanwhile was changing. In the Sun
sides there's space. By contrast RCA added extra
instruments and a vocal group filling in the empty
corners. Gone forever was the spare, revolutionary
sound worked out in Memphis. But, despite this, his
style – for that was what it was becoming – rarely
seems forced. It was always his imitators who
sounded contrived. From 'Heartbreak Hotel'
onwards, Elvis towered over all of pop music.

But he wasn't alone. While other singers younger
than he were inspired by his RCA records, already in
the south 'the rockabilly singers were coming out of
the swamps'.

Carl Perkins   Well, it's one for the money,
Two for the show,
Three to get ready –
Now go, cat, go!
But don't you step on my blue suede shoes . . .

Late 1954 Carl: 'Elvis had just come out with a song, 'That's All Right Mama', and it was exactly the type of thing I was playing.' So, all crammed into the only car they had that was good enough to make the journey, Carl and his band set off to see Sam Phillips. Carl knew his songs were good, but, more than that, his guitar-playing was like Scotty Moore's, fusing blues and fluid country lines.

> White music, I liked Bill Monroe, his fast stuff; for colored, I liked John Lee Hooker, Muddy Waters, their electric stuff. Even back then I liked to do Hooker songs Bill Monroe style, blues with a country beat.

Sam reckoned that, now he'd found Elvis, he didn't need anyone else doing the same thing. But when he sold Elvis to RCA he turned back to Carl, 'said I could record the stuff I like to do. So on Dec. 17 1955 I wrote 'Blue Suede Shoes'. Recorded it Dec. 19, and it was released January 1 1956.'

Carl Perkins became the first white southern rock'n'roller to reach the American pop Top Twenty. 'Blue Suede Shoes' got there just one week before 'Heartbreak Hotel'.

Bad luck followed. On the way to New York for a TV show, the band's car hit a truck. Several months in hospital put them out of the race when it had hardly begun – and Carl's brother Jay later died from his injuries. That accident, at such a crucial time, harmed Carl's career, but

> anyway, Elvis had the looks on me. The girls were going for him for more reasons than music. Elvis was hittin' 'em with sideburns, flashy clothes, and no ring on that finger. I had three kids. There was no way of keeping Elvis from being the man in that music. I've never felt bitter, always felt lucky

being in the music business at all. Most kids from my background never drive a new car.

'Blue Suede Shoes' was the only big hit Carl ever had. Why then do many regard him as the real King of Rock'n'Roll?

Partly it's his guitar work. With Chuck Berry and Scotty Moore he virtually defined rock'n'roll guitar. His playing always matched the character of his songs: individually played notes ('one-string Perkins'), harsh and tense yet melodic as well. His influence was out of all proportion to what little chart success he had.

His songs are the other reason. He wrote them himself and often they tell of his own life. They capture vividly the power of rock'n'roll and the excitement of being young. Writer Greil Marcus has said such songs make you feel Saturday night out could last the whole week through. It's a good description of rock'n'roll itself. Ronnie Hawkins called the bars and clubs where he, Carl and other rockabilly singers used to play, places where 'you had to show your razor and puke twice before they'd let you in.' Here's Carl singing about them:

Now Dan got happy and he started ravin'
He jerked out his razor but he wasn't shavin'
And all the cats knew to jump and hop
'Cos he was born and raised in a butcher's shop –
He hollered 'Rave on, chillen, I'm with ya,
Rave on, cats,' he cried.
'It's almost dawn and the cops are gone,
Let's all get Dixie Fried!'

The idea for 'Blue Suede Shoes' came from 'seeing kids by the bandstand so proud of their new city shoes – you gotta be real poor to care about

Older and more thoughtful – Carl Perkins in the 1960s

new shoes like I did.' The record caught the excitement of the new times. You heard that and Presley's echoed voice in 'Heartbreak Hotel' and the world of pop pap that preceded them blew away in the wind for ever.

Jerry Lee Lewis

Either be hot or cold. If you are lukewarm, the Lord will spew you forth from His mouth.

Jerry Lee Lewis

On stage, his short, wavy blond hair pushed back with a quick sweep of the comb he always carried in his back pocket, raising his hands clear of the keys

BREATHLESS

Words and Music by OTIS BLACKWELL

RECORDED BY
JERRY LEE LEWIS
ON LONDON RECORDS

ABERBACH (LONDON) LTD
142, Charing Cross Road, London, W.C.2.

2/-

Jerry Lee on the
cover of the
sheet music of
his third Top Ten
hit in a row,
spring 1958

to emphasise the chords he was hitting, Jerry Lee
was in complete control. He would lift his right leg
and hit top notes with his foot, leap on top of the
piano and keep the beat going with his heels. His
voice was so expressive, his piano-playing so

distinctive – he was a one-man show. Like all the great rock'n'rollers he didn't sing a song as the old crooners did – he spoke directly to you.

> Open up-a honey, it's your lover-boy me that's
>   knockin'
> Why don't you listen to me, sugar,
> All the cats are at the High School boppin'.
> Honey get your rockin' shoes,
> 'Fore the jukebox blows a fuse –
> Everybody hoppin', everybody boppin',
> Boppin' at the High School Hop.

On record he was just as powerful.

> Well, you see, I always liked Moon Mullican,
> Merrill Moore, a lot of them old boogie woogie
> piano players, I never knew who half of them were
> . . . And I used to hear people like B. B. King too,
> blues singers, I never did know their names.

He heard country music and gospel too, even attending bible school for a while. What he made of all those influences was unique. The left hand pumps out the rhythm while the right stops, starts, pounds out a one-finger, one-note beat, or turns over to let his thumbnail slide again and again down the keys in a flurry of notes.

The tension and power of songs like 'Great Balls Of Fire' comes from feeling that, any moment now, the whole thing might career out of control. But it never does. 'You shake my nerves and you rattle my brain', and then four slammed piano chords as punctuation before 'Too much love drives a man insane/ You broke my will/ But what a thrill' – his voice rises in little, high jumps – 'Goodness gracious! Great balls of fire!' as the drums and left hand crash in at full tilt!

In Presley, Perkins and Lewis, Sam Phillips had three of the greatest rock'n'rollers. Elvis was the one he'd been looking for, but Carl Perkins was a better musician, while Jerry Lee mixed black and white styles on the piano rather than the guitar.

Meanwhile other record companies watched Elvis's amazing success and decided they too needed some of this new southern rock'n'roll. First off the mark was Capitol – through no particular foresight of their own they came up with an original straightaway: Gene Vincent.

Gene Vincent – 'the screaming end'

Gene came from Norfolk, Virginia, over on the east coast, and at the age of seventeen joined the US Navy. But when a car hit his motorbike, crushing his left leg, he was invalided out. The injury troubled him for the rest of his life. Early on when his leg was in plaster it's said he took so little notice of it on stage that the wound would open and blood seep through the cast.

Capitol Records signed Gene and the Bluecaps and moved fast. The week 'Heartbreak Hotel' hit the top of the charts they were recording 'Be Bop A Lula' and 'Woman Love'. Elvis's records used echo and so did Gene's – but through force of circumstance another effect was achieved. Gene's soft voice was at first drowned as the band played full out as if on stage. So

they separated each musician with circular boards so that they were each in a circle by themselves and Gene Vincent was put in another room completely, a little hallway out in the back with headphones so that he could hear what the boys were doing.

The resulting separation was amazing yet all

Gene Vincent   controlled into one tight sound.

Throughout the summer of 1956 'Be Bop A Lula' was in the charts, and the Bluecaps frantically played one-nighters across the United States. As Elvis's outward image became smoother, Gene and Jerry Lee stayed wild and uninhibited. It was partly because their wildness was unacceptable to white middle-class standards of entertainment that their careers suffered in the later 1950s. For the moment, though, the bands of Gene Vincent, Carl Perkins and Elvis made up the first real working rock'n'roll groups.

More rhythm'n'blues was selling to white audiences too. From this upsurge came the three major black rock'n'roll performers: Fats Domino, Chuck Berry and Little Richard.

Fats Domino

'Fats, how'd this rock'n'roll all get started anyway?'
'Well, what you call rock'n'roll now is
rhythm'n'blues. I been playing it for fifteen years in
New Orleans.'

And so he had. From 'They call/ They call me the
Fat Man/ 'Cos I weigh two hundred pounds . . .' in
1949 through 'Blueberry Hill' to the early 1960s,
Fats's lazy style of singing and rolling boogie-piano
backed by horns, sax and drums characterised the
music of New Orleans. He and New Orleans r'n'b
didn't alter style to meet rock'n'roll – the young
rock'n'roll audience came to them. Other forms of
black music had moved north and west as musicians
travelled to find work, but in New Orleans a
distinctive r'n'b sound flourished to become hugely
influential in rock'n'roll first through Fats Domino.

In 1955 Fats's 'Ain't That A Shame' was at the top
of the r'n'b charts, but this was not unusual for him.
What made it so different was that, despite a lame
cover version by Pat Boone, Fats's original climbed
the pop charts too. There were some changes made
to fit the pop market, but they were more of
emphasis than style: trumpeter Dave Bartholomew
who led and arranged for Fats's band could see
which way pop tastes were heading. The overall
sound was crisper, and the hook lines needed to
keep a song in the memory were there too.

'Blueberry Hill' was his biggest hit. Bartholomew
wasn't convinced at first: 'When I first heard the
record, Lew Chudd [head of Fats's record company,
Imperial] asked me what did I think and I said it was
horrible, pull it off the streets fast, you're gonna ruin
Fats.' It did have a pop feel, which was
Bartholomew's objection, but it was still recognisably
r'n'b, the piano echoing each line of the song in a

opposite
Fats Domino at
the piano and
Dave
Bartholomew
working on an
arrangement in
the studio, 1956

gospel call-and-response fashion.

Like Louis Jordan, Fats sang clearly. Though there was no threat in his music, there was warmth and humour. He never set the world alight the way other rock'n'rollers did – he really remained an r'n'b artist. But behind everything else in the 1950s there was always a Fats Domino record rocking irrepressibly along as if he would go on forever despite what happened to anyone else.

Chuck Berry

Roll over Beethoven
And dig those rhythm'n'blues.

Chuck Berry had been a hairdresser in St Louis, Missouri, and had led his own trio for some years. In 1955 he made the familiar pilgrimage to Chicago where Muddy Waters introduced him to Chess Records. His musical experience didn't just include the country blues of the south – he'd been influenced by the quieter night-club blues of Nat King Cole and by Louis Jordan too. At Chess he recorded the first of his famous car songs, 'Maybellene'.

As I was motorvatin' over the hill,
I saw Maybellene in a Coup de Ville,
A Cadillac rollin' on the open road,
Nothin'll outrun my V8 Ford.

In blues the car has often been used as a sexual metaphor – using the idea of a powerful car without actually mentioning that it's sex you're really singing about. But Chuck's songs celebrated the car itself: certainly as a symbol of sex, but also of affluence and speed and, in the America of the 1950s, a teenage daydream. To own a car, cut down and hotted up, meant mobility, energy and flash, listening to rock'n'roll on the radio while you went cruising

opposite
'You can't catch me' – Chuck Berry

looking for girls to impress. Chuck's songs caught this mood.

He too sang clearly rather than in the usually more slurred blues style. His guitar-playing mixed r'n'b riffs with sometimes almost country-picked runs and phrases. Along with Carl Perkins his was the most distinctive playing of the 1950s and his chords, licks and solos have been learnt by nearly every rock guitarist since – a central part of rock'n'roll.

Although he had few big hits at the time, many of his songs have become classics. 'Maybellene' was the biggest of his car songs but I always thought 'You Can't Catch Me' was the best with its almost film-like detail:

New Jersey turnpike in the wee, wee hours,
I was rolling slowly 'cos of drizzling showers,
Here come a flat-top he was moving up with me,
Then come waving goodbye in a little old souped-
   up Jidney.
I put my foot in my tank and I began to roll –
Moanin' siren: it was the State Patrol –
So I let out my wings and then I blew my horn,
Bye-bye New Jersey, I become airborne –
Now you can't catch me . . .

Above all Chuck on record meant the joy and fun of being young and having rock'n'roll to channel it all. On stage, he would crouch down over one heel, the other leg straight out in front of him and, still playing, hop from one side of the stage to the other in his famous 'duck-walk'. And yet there was the paradox of this nearly thirty-year-old black blues singer at the centre of rock'n'roll writing songs about the white American dream of affluence. Although it was obvious that he felt genuinely glad to be 'where hamburgers sizzle on an open grill night and day/

Yeah, and the jukebox jumpin' with records back in the USA,' you were never quite sure he wasn't being ironic as well.

Little Richard   I came from a family where my people didn't like rhythm and blues. Bing Crosby, 'Pennies From Heaven', Ella Fitzgerald was all I heard. And I knew there was something that could be louder than that, but I didn't know where to find it. And I found it was me.

If the heart of rock'n'roll was chaotic and wild, then Little Richard Penniman was both. A contract with Specialty Records brought him to New Orleans. 'I was in Macon, Georgia, washing dishes at the bus-station and I was glad to get out of there.'

14 September 1955 his first session was almost over when someone suggested he record an obscene song he'd been humming. Quickly cleaned up, in three takes 'Tutti Frutti' was cut. Pat Boone covered it but made it just a song. Richard's original was a totally unexpected, violent assault.

AWOP-BOP-ALOOBOP-ALOP-BAM-BOOM
TUTTI FRUTTI, AW ROOTIE . . .

White listeners recoiled. Writer Peter Guralnick remembers hearing it on the way to school: 'Somebody's father was driving, and he expressed our discomfort before we could ourselves. What command of the English language, he said and switched stations. We all laughed self-consciously because it was, after all, our fault.'

'GOT A GAL NAMED SUE/ SHE KNOWS JUST WHAT TO DO . . .' What it said wasn't sexual, but the way he sang it certainly was.

He looked bizarre: hair combed up inches above

Little Richard in the film *The Girl Can't Help It*

his forehead, small moustache, huge grin and wide eyes. He dressed in long jacket and baggy trousers that flapped around his ankles as, standing up at the piano, he would lift one leg straight out like Jerry Lee to bang the notes with his heel. His records were one raw, shouted scream, piano hammering somewhere and a wild sax solo screeching in vain but never topping his singing. He made even the thought of white cover versions impossible. 'On "Long Tall Sally" we upped the tempo and we got the words going so fast that Pat Boone couldn't get his mouth together to do it.' 'Rip It Up', 'The Girl Can't Help It', 'Keep A-Knockin', 'Good Golly Miss Molly' – almost every single he made was a classic.

However, in 1957, on tour in Australia, a fire broke out on his plane and he fell to his knees praying for salvation. When the plane landed safely, that was it. He pledged his life to God, gave up the sinful ways of rock'n'roll, and in a typically extravagant gesture threw his jewelled rings into Sydney Harbour to seal the bargain. For seven years he was an evangelist, returning to rock'n'roll in the wake of the Beatles who'd been partly inspired by him. But though he's produced some good records and his performances are more indulgent than ever, he's never recaptured that first extraordinary power. Perhaps it's as much the fault of changing times as anything else. He resembles the boxer Mohammed Ali – always the self-styled champion. Little Richard has always called himself the 'King of Rock'n'Roll'. Listen to those records he made for Specialty and it's easy to forget there was ever any other contender for the title.

Meanwhile, in rockabilly...

Most record companies tried to produce some rockabilly, even if it was only country with a rock'n'roll beat. At the extremes, both country star Webb Pierce and r'n'b singer Roy Brown recorded in a rockabilly style, neither very successfully. Matching the development of rock'n'roll, rockabilly moved quickly from amplified acoustic to electric guitars, heavier drumming and a less spontaneous sound. Within three years of Elvis's first Sun record, the rockabilly explosion was over, absorbed into city rock'n'roll and back into country music.

There were very few female rock'n'rollers – generally it was country music they came from. Wanda Jackson later sang a handful of wild rockers like her version of Elvis's 'Party' and Janice Martin's best was a sort of tribute, 'My Boy Elvis'. The most successful was Brenda Lee, only eleven years old in

1956. Her voice belied her age and her tiny figure. It could be tough and harsh on rock'n'roll like 'Jambalaya' and 'Let's Jump The Broomstick', and achingly emotional on the ballads which brought her greatest success after the 1950s were over. But, though she got close, none of them could match the rougher r'n'b of black singers like Ruth Brown and Laverne Baker.

Dozens of artists made fine records without ever achieving more than local success. Many, like Warren Smith and Charlie Feathers, became figures of legend. They both came to London in 1977 for a show at the Rainbow Theatre. It must have been the biggest audience either man had ever faced. Both then in their forties they weren't prepared for the hero's welcome awaiting them. When Warren walked on stage to open the show, the entire audience rose to its feet to cheer his being there at all.

And in rhythm'n' blues . . .

Although rock'n'roll opened the door to a wider market, it was usually the less black-sounding records which became hits in the pop charts.

From Chess came two artists who were a vital part of rock'n'roll. Chuck Berry, of course, was one. The other was Bo Diddley. He claimed to have invented his own distinctive rhythm – the pounding 'shave-and-a-haircut/ two bits' – so called because those words spoken aloud sound most like the guitar/ drums/maraccas-led beat. Where Berry's guitar sounded, as he sang in 'Johnny B. Goode', 'just like a-ringin' a bell', Diddley's playing was rougher and distortedly loud. He called his biggest hit 'Bo Diddley' after himself. The infectious rhythm, murky vocals and powerful guitar crossed black/white boundaries, establishing him as one of the major rock'n'roll innovators.

opposite
Bo Diddley on the right with 'The Duchess' and Jerome Green on maraccas

Atlantic Records had two of the best song-writers and producers of the time, Jerry Leiber and Mike Stoller. Some of their best work was with the Coasters, who appealed to black audiences as well as white teenagers. The subjects of their songs were often unusual for the pop market. 'Riot In Cell Block No. 9' told of a prison riot led by Scarface Jones – 'It's too late to quit/ Pass the dynamite 'cos the fuse is lit.' Behind the music were wailing police sirens and heavy machine-gun fire. The fine lyrics and the wit of the Coasters' singing helped make such songs great rock'n'roll. Their different voices were used as separate characters in their records. In 'Young Blood', as they spy a beautiful girl, each speaks the line 'Look-a there!' so convincingly you can almost see the gang of them hanging out on the street corner watching as she walks by.

There was another side of r'n'b involved in the success of rock'n'roll. It didn't have a name at the time, but was later called 'doo-wop' after the sounds the group sang behind the lead voice.

Doo-wop   Doo-wop has been called the 'street-corner sound' for, according to legend, this is where groups of black teenagers would gather to sing in the poorer quarters of New York City, Los Angeles and Philadelphia. Resonance and echo could be added by singing in the stairwells of large tenement buildings. Instruments were expensive and unnecessary: instead, different voices could carry lead melody (often taken by a tenor voice), harmonies, and even rhythm parts – hence 'doo-wop', 'oo-bop-shu-wah', 'shoo-doo-n-shoo-be-doo' and a host of others.

Good melodies brought doo-wop into the pop charts. The Chords' 'Sh-Boom', the Crows' 'Gee' and

The Platters in 1955

the Penguins' 'Earth Angel' were the first big hits, and many songs were covered by white artists too. The most successful group was the Platters. However there was a pop slant to their hits 'Only You' and 'The Great Pretender'. Though they were good, they weren't the best example of the style. There were hundreds of groups – some managed one hit and then it was back to the car-lot or the factory production line as record companies dropped them in favour of the next group with a good song. Frankie Lymon and the Teenagers had a number one hit with 'Why Do Fools Fall In Love?' and a newspaper claimed that thirteen-year-old Frankie was 'Rock'n'Rolling to the tune of £50,000 a year'. If

We're not juvenile delinquents – Frankie Lymon (right) and the Teenagers down in the stairwell

so, the Teenagers probably saw little of this money. Frankie was soon back on the streets of New York – and a heroin addict. One cold day in February 1968, forgotten for ten years, he made the front page again. He was found dead of an overdose in his grandmother's apartment. He was twenty-six years old, and, for a moment then, everyone remembered him again.

Conclusion

My Daddy and I were laughing about it the other day. He looked at me and said, 'What happened, El? The last thing I can remember is I was working in a can factory, and you were driving a truck!'

Elvis, 1956

By the middle of 1957 the first tidal wave of rock'n'roll was well on its way. At the beginning the big record companies like RCA and Capitol realised something was happening but they didn't know what it was. Unlike Sun and the other small companies where it began, they were neither young nor flexible enough, nor close to the roots. As for understanding rock'n'roll, all they could see was that in pop music terms Elvis had star quality, but they weren't prepared for the explosion of rock'n'roll and the demands of the new young audience – an audience they were only just beginning to respond to. Pop deals with product, selling records, not with something like the vast youth movement and sense of revolt which lay behind rock'n'roll. Pop can only cope with such things when it has learnt how best to make money from them. Pop is business.

Meanwhile rock'n'roll's success wasn't confined to the United States.

7 Rock island line: Britain in the mid-1950s

'Teenager' of Birmingham, who asks us not to publish his name and address 'as it may affect my work', writes:

I'm afraid that Miss Kelly who hates the Hit Parade because of 'gimmick records' would be a real wash-out with my crowd. Every Saturday night, a whole crowd of us teenagers gather in sweaters and jeans at my house, where Mum has turned over to me the front room, which she aptly calls The Rock-And-Roll Room. From seven p.m. until midnight the room simply rocks to Bill Haley, Rusty Draper, Fats Domino, Elvis Presley, the Teenagers, and all the horrible, gimmicky records that Miss Kelly refers to. Hot and loud and vulgar music, non-stop for five hours. Luckily my home is detached so there is no fear of complaining neighbours.

The room, contemporary in style, hasn't much furniture. Just a gram, record cabinets, studio couch, an assortment of chairs, and a soft drinks bar. So we push everything to the sides and just rock-and-roll, and suddenly the whole crazy, mixed-up world seems to be put right, alive and new.

It gives me a feeling that's hard to express in

writing. But on these Saturday nights, when everything is so gay and young, it really feels good to be alive.

Letter to *New Musical Express*, 27 July 1956

Nothing really affected me until Elvis.

John Lennon

In Britain no one had heard anything like Elvis before – there was no British blues or country music tradition. Somehow Elvis's presence on record was so commanding he could even make you appreciate a sentimental old ballad like 'Blue Moon' without feeling too embarrassed at yourself or for him. By Christmas 1956 his first film was showing in London.

As an ardent Elvis Presley fan I have been to see his first screen role in *Love Me Tender*. When he sang his first song, it was quite an experience to sit and watch the audience's reaction. Some laughed at his gyrations, while others gasped and many just looked on in complete embarrassment. I stayed to see a repeat of the film as did many others. For the first ten minutes Elvis did not appear, but at last he came into view ploughing a field. Here came the screamagers, blotting out his first lines, and it continued like this throughout the film. Every movement or speech he made was met by screams of delight, so making it impossible to hear the rest of the film.

This grew even worse when he didn't appear in a scene, for all around were cries of 'Elvis, where are you?' When he sang the audience clapped in time with the tune.

On the way out, I overheard three girls discussing the film. They were among the noisiest in the audience. 'Wasn't he smashing?' they said. I fail to understand how on earth they could tell!

'Puzzled Teenager' from Brixton, *New Musical Express*, 28 December 1956

And rockabilly? Much more has been released in Britain since the 1950s than during them, but Johnny Burnette's Rock'n'Roll Trio could certainly be heard. They sound fresh even today – then, they were shattering.

By 1957, the pop industry was pushing calypso as the craze to follow rock'n'roll – but as usual they'd got it all wrong. At the pictures it was a different story. Presley made the films *Loving You* and *Jailhouse Rock*, and in *Don't Knock the Rock*, starring Bill Haley, Little Richard stole the show. Gene Vincent joined Richard and Fats Domino in *Thee Girl Can't Help It*, and Eddie Cochran sang 'Twenty Flight Rock'. *Disc Jockey Jamboree* went on release with a documentary about James Dean, and introduced Britain to Jerry Lee Lewis's 'Great Balls Of Fire'.

But what about the effect of all this on British bands and singers? Was there any British rock'n'roll? The answer is yes, and though much of it was rather poor, some was very good indeed.

Britain's bands try to rock'n'roll – 'Shortnin' Bread Rock'

How many of the dance-hall dandies loafing on the edge of the floor can really dance? They jive to every quickstep – and annoy decent dancers – and whenever a slow number is played they just hug their partners and shuffle round the hall.

Dancer, Corsham, Wilts.

In the dance-halls in 1956 the big orchestras played plodding versions of rock'n'roll numbers. But newer bands like Art Baxter's Rockin' Sinners started up.

Some were offshoots of jazz or dance bands. Mostly they were inspired by Bill Haley, and many made a fatal mistake. For years bands had kept up with the latest crazes by modifying what they'd always played. When the mambo was popular it was easy to change to a mambo rhythm, perhaps adding a bit of Latin-American percussion, and the dancers in the halls kept on dancing. But rock'n'roll wasn't just another dance craze: it was a radical break with the past. It required a musical experience that was foreign to British musicians. One of the worst backings ever is on Tommy Steele's 'Rock With The Caveman'. Yet though the musicians were experienced jazzmen, they neither could nor wanted to play rock'n'roll.

A lot of what the first bands served up sounded lame beside the American originals but they at least provided contact with live rock'n'roll. And things were beginning to change. Many dance-halls allowed rock'n'roll, but jiving was forbidden! Yet by the end of 1956 this ban was starting to be lifted. In December the Locarno Ballroom in Leeds began lunchtime rock'n'roll sessions: admission 3d (one new penny)!

However the road for would-be rock'n'rollers wasn't via the dance bands but through a do-it-yourself music called skiffle. It was close enough to rock'n'roll in some ways not to matter too much if the real thing wasn't around.

Skiffle   And as I look around me,
I'm sometimes apt to smile,
Seeing all the young folks
Putting on the style.

Lonnie Donegan, 1957

The first skiffle hit happened almost by accident. There'd been a revival of traditional jazz in the early 1950s and several bands included a skiffle session as an interlude. The music dated from the 1920s when groups would form at Chicago parties to raise money for rent. They would play whatever was lying around that would make a musical noise: jugs, bottles and home-made double basses. In 1954 the skiffle group in Chris Barber's Band recorded an old song 'Rock Island Line' about a toll-gate keeper being fooled by train-drivers smuggling through goods on which they should have paid a high customs duty. When the train was safely past, the driver would 'shout back to the man down the line/ I fooled you, I fooled you/ I got pig-iron, I got all pig-iron.' Lonnie Donegan sang the song and afterwards he probably forgot all about it until radio request programmes were flooded by postcards from listeners wanting to hear it. Released as a single while 'Rock Around The Clock' was at Number One in January 1956, Lonnie Donegan's 'Rock Island Line' rocketed into the Top Ten.

The timing was crucial, for it got caught up in the rush for rock'n'roll. In no time at all there were hundreds of skiffle groups all over Britain. It was easy and cheap and everyone tried to do it. All you needed was a washboard and thimbles for the ends of your fingers to scrape against its corrugated ridges, and a double bass. You made it from an old tea-chest (more plentiful then), with a broom-handle fixed to one corner and a piece of string stretched from the top of the handle to the opposite bottom corner of the chest. Finally, you needed an acoustic guitar, the most important instrument and the most expensive, but it wasn't beyond a collection of saved-up pocket money. As the craze grew it became easier to buy one on the new hire-purchase scheme: so much down and so much per week, hopefully out of what you earned playing it. Like rock'n'roll, skiffle was basic, vital and brash – and played on the same instruments.

Lonnie Donegan   All I set out to be was a banjo-player in a jazz band.

It was Donegan who became the King of Skiffle. From 1956 to the early 1960s his records were rarely out of the charts. Other groups copied his success. Wally Whyton's Vipers, Chas McDevitt and Nancy Whiskey, and Johnny Duncan all had hits. Duncan called his band The Bluegrass Boys: their 'Last Train To San Fernando' was in fact more country than blues. Lonnie combined both. He adapted folk-blues such as the songs of Huddie 'Leadbelly' Ledbetter, country numbers and Woody Guthrie songs.

I picked songs that were, for example, Leadbelly songs, but also songs that could be understood not just by some old spade in the cotton-fields sixty years ago, but also by the tram-driver in East Ham High Street.

In his own way he was pulling together much the same strands as the rock'n'rollers.

I formed skiffle clubs in all the major cities as opposed to fan clubs. I wanted to encourage the appreciation of Afro-American folk music. So we used to hold meetings and give a talk and a lecture and play them a few songs, and help them to form a group with a few tips.

Some critics were quick to accuse him of selling out his principles, taking a pure music into show-business. In fact, Lonnie showed that music-making

Lonnie Donegan (centre-stage) on the set of '6.5 Special'

need not be confined to professional musicians where only years of practice and skill would make you accepted. He inspired the first mass musical movement in Britain. From skiffle came nearly all the 1950s' rock'n'roll and pop singers and many of the groups of the mid-1960s. They were fired as much by Lonnie as by the American rock'n'rollers. His influence has often been unappreciated. Without him there would have been no skiffle boom – and without skiffle there would have been precious little British rock'n'roll.

In the end, however, skiffle was a bit too respectable, too much like folk music with its acoustic guitars strumming cheerily away. Youth clubs welcomed skiffle, but hated rock'n'roll and Teddy boys. There were several suspicious attempts by earnest young vicars to present skiffle services in their churches. Meanwhile, rock'n'roll increasingly reflected teenage lifestyles while skiffle was still dealing with freight trains and taking water to cotton-picking field-hands. You didn't see much of that sort of thing in south London around the Elephant and Castle way.

Through the coffee-bars to rock'n'roll

Well I got a girl with a record machine,
When it comes to rockin' she's the queen,
I love to dance on a Saturday night,
All alone I can hold her tight,
But she lives on the twentieth floor uptown –
The elevator's broken down.

So I walked one, two flights, three flights, four,
Five, six, seven flights, eight flights more,
Up on the twelfth it's getting a drag,
Fifteenth floor I'm starting to sag –
Get to the top, I'm too tired to rock.

> Eddie Cochran, 'Twenty Flight Rock'

Up in Liverpool, John Lennon's skiffle group was soon learning to play rock'n'roll songs like 'Twenty Flight Rock'. Skiffle was a means to an end – a good apprenticeship but a stopgap until rock'n'roll could be learned and electric instruments afforded. The way to be 'spotted' by record companies on the lookout for British Elvises was to play at one of the new coffee-bar/clubs. By 1958 there were over 4000 of them, although very few had a stage and live entertainment. Italian in inspiration, they seemed ultra-modern with their plastic and tubular steel furniture and bamboo partitions. They were dominated by the flashing lights of space-age Wurlitzer jukeboxes and fruit-machine-handled, chrome-plated coffee-machines hissing forth *cappucinos* into glass cups. Jet Harris of the Shadows remembers the most famous one.

I went to the Two I's coffee-bar to sell coffee and Coke. I was paid a few bob a night there. In odd moments I would play bass in the cellar, learning and improving all the time. The Two I's was like an unofficial agency for rock'n'roll musicians seeking work. Singers in search of musicians would often drop in and offer someone a job.

It was from the Two I's in the autumn of 1956 that Tommy Steele leapt to fame.

Tommy Steele

I was fortunate enough to see Tommy Steele at Sunderland Empire last week. He's terrific. The Pelvis hasn't got a look in. From now on it's Tommy, not Elvis, for me!
Letter in *New Musical Express*, 16 November 1956

Tommy was a merchant seaman and had learned a lot of blues and country music that was new to Britain. So when he sang at the Two I's he already had a sizeable repertoire of songs.

There were three things the coffee bars offered someone of, say, seventeen or eighteen. They offered you one spaghetti and egg meal in the evening, which was vital. You were allowed to pass the saucer round twice in the evening – that's all – which was your bus fare. And third, there was also the promise of the place packed out with birds, which was very essential to a seventeen-year-old, especially if he was a budding musician. You gotta feed on something.

Enter John Kennedy, a publicist from New Zealand, who persuaded him on the spot to go into show-business.

And there and then, as the empty cups piled up on

Early 1957:
Tommy Steele
and the Steelmen
– and one of the
amps and
speakers that
worried the
theatres

the table, I told him my plans. I said that rock'n'roll music had got a bad name from Teddy Boy hooligans who wrecked cinemas and broke up cafes. But it was coming to Europe nonetheless. It would get bigger and anyone who went along with it would himself grow big on the crest of its wave.

'But someone has got to lift it out of its Teddy Boy rut, give it class and get society as well as the thousands of ordinary decent kids singing and dancing it. I know the publicity business if I know nothing else. With your voice and personality and my publicity I'm certain we can do it. What about it?'

He stirred his tea, looking down into his cup thoughtfully. Then he pushed his hand across the table.

Tommy Steele at
The Cat's
Whisker Club

'Alright, Johnny mate, I'll tell you what I'll do. I'm going back to sea in a fortnight. I'll do what you tell me until then. If we get anywhere I'll stay on. If we don't, then you've had me, mate.'

It was a crowded two weeks. Kennedy fooled the Press into giving Tommy maximum coverage. There was a specially arranged party which reporters were hoodwinked into believing was crammed with the sons and daughters of the very rich, all crazy about East Ender Tommy and rock'n'roll. And there was the rigged photograph of the Duke of Kent supposedly leaving a Soho club where he'd been specially to hear Tommy. Within a month, his first record was in the Top Twenty. Tommy had become the first in a line of 'answers-to-Elvis' that was to lead right up to Cliff Richard.

But only Tommy's first two records were attempts

at rock'n'roll. By Christmas he was heading for Number One with 'Singing The Blues', still the song most associated with him. But it wasn't rock'n'roll. A career in stage-shows, films and television lay ahead. It was clear that he was developing into an all-round entertainer. For if he didn't appeal to those who only wanted raw rock'n'roll, he was certainly welcomed by nearly everyone else.

The first serious challenger to Tommy as Britain's number one teen sensation was Terry Dene.

Terry Dene

One week I was a quiet boy with no girl-friends, a non-drinker who earned £4 a week and went to bed early. The next, I was pocketing £30 or more, being mobbed by hundreds of fans. There were parties and late nights, there was booze and flattery.

The agent who found Terry singing in the Two I's told him: 'We're going to fix your hair and teeth, and soon we'll have your name in lights!' In 1957 Terry's name was indeed in lights. He had hit records and made a film with a pretty corny story-line about British rock'n'roll – *The Golden Disc*. But from there it was all downhill. His difficulties were made worse by an entertainment industry uninterested in Terry but determined to make money from the new goldmine of rock'n'roll.

The final straw came when Terry's National Service call-up papers arrived. Elvis had just been called up too, and the US Army had made the most of all the publicity. So when Terry arrived at Winchester Barracks, the British Army tried to do the same.

Several times he strode backwards and forwards through the barrack gate; then a Press officer

Terry Dene
arrives at
Winchester
Barracks

suggested that the media men should adjourn to the mess and shoot movie pictures. They clamoured for vantage points as Terry collected his pie and mash and sat down at a table. Almost before he had finished his meal, he was rushed to the quarter-master's stores to be kitted out. 'Just one more shot, Terry!' 'Could you do it again?'

Terry couldn't do it again. Within a couple of days he had a nervous breakdown. Soon he was a civilian with a shattered singing career and details of his personal life common knowledge in the Press.

His records sound more dated today than most, but he made some brave stabs at rock'n'roll which might still stand up were it not for the musical backings straight out of a past era of popular music. Sometimes it sounded as if Terry was in one studio singing rock songs while an orchestra and chorus were in another playing something quite different.

And so it often was. Tommy Steele remembers the mid-1950s shows he played at. It was the old music-hall/variety show system in theatres which were much happier with comedians, jugglers and acrobats than young men with electric guitars.

We'd bring the amps in – and they'd never seen amps. They'd *never* seen amps! And you'd start setting this stuff up and the Fire Department would come round and say 'What is that?' and you'd say 'It's an electric amplifier . . .' 'Electric??! D'you mean you're bringing live stuff on apart from the microphone belonging to the theatre?! . . .' And so we used to end up in every city having to pay for a fireman to stand on each side of the theatre, by the stage; and we had to put, at the side of each amp, a big red bucket with 'FIRE' written on it, full of sand.

Meanwhile, the Two I's and other clubs boomed as group after group got hold of electric instruments and tried their hand at rock'n'roll – or at least at music with a beat. For to the pop music industry even the name 'rock'n'roll' was embarrassing. It much preferred to talk about the 'big beat' and 'beat music' – that way it hoped people wouldn't be put off by rock'n'roll's Teddy boy ancestry.

But Cliff Richard had seen Bill Haley at the Edmonton Granada, and Marty Wilde was determined to copy Terry Dene's success. They both idolised Elvis, and, with Billy Fury and Johnny Kidd, they were to be the next chapter in Britain's attempts to rock'n'roll.

8 Back in the USA: America in the late 1950s

Elvis romantically recreating his Army days in the film *G.I. Blues*, 1960

Monday 24 March 1958   Memphis. Elvis becomes a US Army National Serviceman. For the next two years he will be officially known as military number US53310761. Pressmen and newsreel cameras record his every move as he is medically examined,

fitted with his uniform, and, to the glee of the older generation everywhere, receives an army haircut – no more sideburns and no more grease!

And then on Friday March 28 Elvis and eighteen other buck privates boarded a bus at dawn for the 425-mile trip to the middle of Texas. No, the Army was sorry. It couldn't release the names of towns and restaurants where the bus would stop. Security, you know. Security against the 'enemy' – teenagers.

Soon Elvis was off to an Army camp in Germany, and in came a second wave of rock'n'rollers a few years younger.

Buddy Holly and the Crickets

Well, that'll be the day
When you say goodbye,
Yes, that'll be the day
When you make me cry,
Yes, that'll be the da-a-ay
When I die . . .

Buddy Holly's music perhaps best bridges the gap between rock'n'roll and the best of 1960s' pop. His deep influence was felt by the Beatles and even Bob Dylan and is still important today. Yet he died in a plane crash less than eighteen months after his first hit.

Coming from west Texas he felt that area's wide range of blues and country influences. Seeing Elvis on stage, in 1955, had a profound effect. His hillbilly music changed to his own rockabilly style. Late in the summer of 1957 the mixture of his influences and Jerry Allison's drumming sent 'That'll Be The Day' straight to the top on both sides of the Atlantic.

Holly mixed lead and rhythm on one guitar and

'Rave On' –
Buddy Holly, his
Fender
Stratocaster, and
the Crickets

with bass and drums what the Crickets produced was a total, indivisible sound. In 'Peggy Sue', for instance, Holly's voice, Allison's constant rolling drums and the strummed rhythm and chopped chords of the lead form one complete whole. He had two recording deals: Brunswick issued Crickets' records with Holly as singer; Coral produced Holly's records with, at first anyway, the Crickets backing him. In 1958 their hits dominated the charts: 'Oh Boy', 'Maybe Baby' and 'Think It Over' by the Crickets; and 'Peggy Sue', 'Listen To Me' and 'Rave On' by Holly.

His voice would jump from high to low and back again depending on the emphasis the words needed.

At times these vocal leaps sounded like a musical hiccup – he gave the single word 'Sue' in 'Peggy Sue' no less than ten syllables stretching it out to the fast beat of the drums. Often his imagination and talent were way ahead of his contemporaries. The breathy phrasing of 'Slippin' And Slidin'' still sounds inventive, while the hesitant, conversational tone of 'Well All Right' makes it one of the most sensitive of all pop songs.

The Crickets, however, weren't willing to go with him when he moved to New York. None the less, his studio experiments continued. From these final sessions 'It Doesn't Matter Any More' was released at the time of his death in early 1959. Instead of the Crickets there was an orchestra behind him. But Holly made creative use of it, neither being swamped, nor ending up like one of the smooth-voiced crooners of the past. The plucked *pizzicato* strings led to hundreds of imitations beginning with John Barry's intelligent arranging of Adam Faith's early British hits and finally plumbing the depths with the overblown sound of later Bobby Vee records.

Buddy himself always seemed a most unlikely rocker. In early photos he looked an ungainly country youth, and in later ones, wearing his heavy-rimmed spectacles, he seemed quiet, easy-going and thoughtful. Almost single-handed he created a new style of pop music grown out of rock'n'roll. More than anyone else, Holly and the Crickets made it on their music.

Eddie Cochran   Sometimes I wonder what I'm a-gonna do,
But there ain't no cure for the summertime blues.

Two years younger than Holly, Eddie Cochran also began with hillbilly but Elvis changed him too. His

family had moved to California when he was eleven
and there he met song-writer Jerry Capehart.
Together they wrote and recorded, Eddie playing all
the guitars, overdubbing himself on tape, and
Capehart sometimes using a cardboard box as a
drumkit.

After a performance in *The Girl Can't Help It* came
'Summertime Blues', one of the all-time great
rock'n'roll songs. 'Of all the seasons there'd never
been a blues about summer,' said Capehart. 'C'mon
Everybody' and 'Somethin' Else' followed and they
reflect the world of the American High School
teenager better than anything else. The standpoint is
Eddie's own, summing up not just excitement –
'Been doing my homework all the week long/ Now
the house is empty and the folks are gone/ Whoo –
c'mon everybody' – but also the frustration of losing
out, of not being as triumphant and dominating as
Elvis always sounded.

> Well, look a-there, there she comes –
> There comes that girl again,
> Wanted to date her since I don't know when,
> But she don't notice me when I pass,
> She goes with all the guys from out-a my class,
> But that can't stop me from a-thinkin' to myself:
> She's sure fine-looking, man,
> She's somethin' else!

Before he died in 1960, he was a bigger star in
Britain than in the United States. Without anyone
knowing very much about him, he turned out some
great rock'n'roll. A fine musician, he never became
one of the late 1950s' teenage idols – there was a
toughness and sense of humour about him that
prevented it. He was his own man. At a time when
pop singers were trying to be the respectable boy-

Eddie Cochran

next-door, Eddie was just one of the gang downtown – not even the leader, just hanging out, taking the knocks of teenage life but always bouncing back again.

> Hey, look a-here, just wait and see,
> Work hard and save my dough,
> I'll buy that car that I been wanting so
> Get me that girl and we'll go ridin' around . . .
> I keep right on a-dreamin' and a-thinkin' to myself:
> If it all comes true, man –
> Wow! That's somethin' else!

Ricky Nelson and the Everly Brothers

Ricky Nelson's parents had a situation-comedy series on TV which starred Ricky too; the Everlys had a country music radio show in Kentucky with their two sons singing along with them. It was a family affair, complete with contacts in the record business.

Nelson would grease his hair, sweep it back and sneer and more than passably resemble Elvis. But he also looked nice enough to appeal to a younger audience who, like their parents, were a bit disturbed by Elvis's apparent wildness. His first hit was a cover of a Fats Domino song that sounded much better than anything the likes of Pat Boone might have turned out. He started out seeing himself as a rockabilly singer: 'I wanted to be Carl Perkins,' he said, 'I wanted the Sun sound.' In his best recordings it shows. His guitarist, James Burton, kept things close to rock'n'roll with a strength and an edge that most of Ricky's contemporaries couldn't manage. Though his phrasing is sometimes a shade too polite to carry the roughness of rock'n'roll, like Cochran he sang fairly accurately of the lifestyles of his suburban teenage audience.

Don and Phil Everly sang in harmony, their high voices stopping just short of being nasal. They sounded very close to the country singing-duo tradition they came from, but their strummed, drum-like guitar chords provided that necessary rock'n'roll rhythm. The titles of the fine teenage love songs they sang seemed to sum up their music: 'All I Have To Do Is Dream', 'Devoted To You', 'Problems', 'When Will I Be Loved'. Their contrasting voices – Phil's soft and romantic, Don's harder and tougher – added drama to songs which would have sounded sickly-sweet in other hands – and frequently did! It wasn't rockabilly, it was country moved near to teenage rock'n'roll.

'They're only singing in thirds,' said a schoolfriend of mine scornfully at the time. At least I think that's what he said for I didn't know what he meant. What I did know was that it was possible to like the wilder men of rock'n'roll and still find a place for the Everlys' country harmonies telling of an ideal world of teenage joy and heartbreak. They certainly didn't possess the flash or rebellion of Elvis or Jerry Lee, but more than anyone except Buddy Holly their pop style bridged 1950s' and 1960s' pop. Their influence can be directly heard in the Beatles and, most tellingly, the Byrds. By comparison, of course, Presley and the first rock'n'rollers sang with an emotion and a fire that was almost adult. The Everlys, and Holly, Cochran and Nelson too, sounded less knowing – more innocent. They and their music were much more comfortable for a younger audience to identify with, yet still had one of the great strengths of rock'n'roll: they spoke directly to their audience.

opposite
The Everly
Brothers

'You say that music's for the birds . . .'

You say that music's for the birds,
And you can't understand the words,
But honey if you did
You'd really blow your lid
'Cos baby that is rock'n'roll.

The Coasters

A good song, one that sells, is one that the mass of people can associate with, that says something they've felt.

Carl Perkins

Many pre-rock'n'roll popular songs were slight, schmaltzy and unrealistic. They spoke of perfect love and settling down in a forever world of 'roses-round-the-cottage-door'. John Shepherd's *Tin Pan Alley* gives a fuller analysis of songs and lyrics of this pre-rock'n'roll period. But, in a nutshell, the guiding principles were:

   (i) no offence should be given;
  (ii) it's only entertainment;
 (iii) any reference to sex, however obscure, was smutty, obscene and dirty-minded.

'Love and marriage', sang Frank Sinatra, 'go together like a horse and carriage.'

The first white rock'n'roll by Bill Haley followed the same pattern: 'We steer completely clear of anything suggestive,' he said, and he meant it. Joe Turner's original 'Shake Rattle and Roll' opened with 'Get out of that bed/ And wash your face and hands' and went on:

Well you wear low dresses,
The sun comes shinin' through,
I can't believe my eyes
That all of this belongs to you.

Haley's version starts in the kitchen, not the bedroom ('Get out in that kitchen/ And rattle those pots and pans'), and the unacceptable 'low dresses' are made decent:

> You wear those dresses,
> Your hair done up so nice,
> You look so warm
> But your heart is cold as ice.

It's a different woman entirely. Haley played it safe. At first, Elvis probably never gave it much thought. In Tupelo and Memphis he'd grown up hearing blues and r'n'b. When he sang 'Shake Rattle and Roll' he made no changes to the original. Haley wasn't outrageous and offensive to white middle-class standards – Elvis was. But it would be wrong to place too much emphasis on suggestive lyrics as the cause of the outrage. After all, Little Richard got away with a fairly plain reference to adultery in 'Long Tall Sally' but that was probably because you couldn't hear the words clearly anyway.

> Well I saw Uncle John
> With Long Tall Sally,
> He saw Aunt Mary comin'
> So he ducked back in the alley.

A lot of people couldn't understand Elvis's words either, but because of the way he looked and the tone of his singing they expected them to be undesirable and dirty.

Even so there was no room for bringing too much out in the open. It was still the 1950s – there wasn't that much permissiveness. The older generation was concerned about teenagers' lack of morals, but you wouldn't have guessed there was much immorality from the majority of hit songs. When the Everlys and their date fall asleep during a movie that 'wasn't so hot': they're genuinely worried about her parents' reaction to their being late:

Wake up little Susie and weep,
The movie's over, it's four o'clock,
And we're in trouble deep.

Even Elvis changed Smiley Lewis's original 'One Night of Sin' to 'One Night with You'. In any case the words were beside the point: the meaning came over in the sound of the records. It was the energy and intent behind it that mattered. The way Gene Vincent sang 'Woman Love' left no room for thinking he meant just holding hands. Like Johnnie Ray, what came over was real feeling, not shallow sentimentality. The words didn't always state what was meant. If asked at the time for the words of Little Richard's 'Tutti Frutti' you might have been able to repeat only the chorus: 'Awop-bop-aloo-bop-alop-bam-boom/ Tutti frutti/ Aw rootie . . .' If the older generation insisted this proved that rock'n'roll was meaningless and therefore dangerous, you could only reply with the truth: 'No – it proves nothing of the sort. It's what I feel listening to the whole thing that matters. That's the meaning. You can't see it, because you don't feel what I feel.'

Rock'n'roll was a teenage music and lyrics came to deal with teenage concerns: school, dating and the joys and troubles of young love, clothes, cars, jukeboxes, rock'n'roll itself, and the restrictions that parents and others could place on you. Chuck Berry had it summed up.

Up in the morning and out to school,
The teacher is teaching the golden rule,
American history and practical math,

You're studying hard and hoping to pass,
Working your fingers right down to the bone –
The guy behind you won't leave you alone.

Ring ring goes the bell,
The cook in the lunchroom's ready to sell.
You're lucky if you can find a seat,
You're fortunate if you have time to eat,
Back in the classroom, open your books,
Bet the teacher don't know how mean she looks.

Soon as three o'clock rolls around,
You finally lay your burden down,
Close up your books, get out of your seat,
Down the hall and into the street,
Up to the corner and round the bend,
Right to the juke-joint you go in.

Drop the coin right into the slot,
You gotta hear something that's really hot,
With the one you love you're making romance,
All day long you've been wanting to dance,
Feeling the music from head to toe
Round and round and round you go.

And maybe if you were lucky you'd meet Chuck's
'Little Queenie':

There she is again standing over by the record
    machine,
Looking like a model on the cover of a
    magazine –
She's too cute to be a minute over seventeen.

Though the music was aggressive, the feelings
expressed still sounded pretty conventional: 'Won't
you wear my ring/ Around your neck/ To tell the
world/ I'm yours by heck!' And meanwhile Ricky
Nelson was singing about things going wrong: 'I bet

she's out having a ball/ Not even thinking of me at all/ Stood up/ Brokenhearted again.'

The best rock'n'roll songs, the ones which meant most were, as Carl Perkins said, those you could identify yourself with. Rock'n'roll reflected the new 1950s' world of the teenager.

Clothes were important – 'Blue Suede Shoes', perhaps, or 'Black Denim Trousers and Motor-Cycle Boots'. So were cars. Here Chuck Berry reigned supreme. Coup de Villes, Cadillacs, a Jaguar and a Thunderbird, the detail of 'they bought a souped-up Jidney, was a cherry-red '53' – he sang about them all. Occasionally there was trouble:

> Everything is wrong since me and my baby parted,
> All day long I'm walking 'cos I couldn't get my car started,
> Laid up on my job and I can't afford to check it,
> I wish somebody'd come along and run into it and wreck it.

But whether it was 'Don'tcha step on my blue suede shoes', 'You can't catch me' or even 'You get your kicks/On route 66' it was all the same idea: fast-moving, enjoying yourself, 'Don't want your botheration/ Get away, leave me.'

Many songs dealt just with the power of rock'n'roll: 'Roll Over Beethoven', 'Just let me hear some of that rock'n'roll music,/ It's got a back-beat, you can't lose it.' 'Send to the store,' sang Elvis, 'Let's buy some more/Let's have a party tonight,' while Eddie Cochran put out a warning: 'Well, we'll really have a party but we gotta put a guard outside/ If the folks come home I'm afraid they're gonna have my hide . . .' For there were restrictions roaming round the edges of this new-found freedom – some were trivial perhaps, but they were keenly felt. There were still 'botherations' even if you were 'Almost Grown':

> Take out the papers and the trash
> Or you don't get no spending cash.
>
> The Coasters

> Workin' in the fillin' station
> Too many tasks,
> 'Wipe the windows, check the tyres,
> Check the oil, uh, a dollar gas.'
> Huh! Too much monkey business
> For me to be involved in.
>
> Chuck Berry

> Car-top down, just ridin' around on a weekend,
> Took a chance on crashin' a dance on a
>   weekend,
> We were almost inside the place
> When somebody slammed the door in my face,
> 'Hey, you guys, you gotta wear ties on a weekend.'
>
> Eddie Cochran

Movin' 'n' groovin'

But rock'n'roll wasn't all singing – there were instrumental groups too. Mostly they centred on guitarists: of them all, the most successful was Duane Eddy, but the most influential was Link Wray.

Eddy's records used a primitive echo to boost and deepen the sound of melody lines played on the bass strings of Duane's guitar. 'Twangy' was the word used to describe it. 'Rebel Rouser', in the summer of 1958, was his first big hit. In Britain the tough bass sound, honking saxes and rebel yells brought him great popularity. In 1960 Duane toured Britain with Bobby Darin. It was a great show but a mismatched bill. The Trocadero, at the Elephant and Castle, was full of people who'd come to see Duane and had little patience with Darin's Sinatra-styled act.

'The Guitar Man'
– Duane Eddy

Constantly barracked by the audience, Darin closed the show. He was good, but before he came on, Duane and his Rebels had played so loudly that the walls of the theatre seemed to shake in time to the beat. The difference was plain: Duane was still close to rock'n'roll, Darin had already left it behind.

Link Wray was almost unknown at the time. The heavy bass riff of his growling, sinister 'Rumble' had Link's reverberating tremolo guitar on top amplified almost to distortion. It was rough, crude and powerful – a dirty sound. And as Link recalls, it packed quite a punch, especially one night when a New York gang clustered round the stage: 'Even the cops were scared of 'em. I had to play "Rumble" five times for those guys, y'know. They'd line up against the stage and I'd have to start the number all over again!'

Link's sound directly foreshadowed rock guitar-playing of the 1960s with its better equipment and greater electronic range. But in the end there was less room for such raw, biting rock'n'roll. The cleaner, restrained music of groups like the Ventures became the standard sound. They were the American equivalent of Britain's top early 1960s group the Shadows. Highly competent and excellent in their way, the Shadows' 'Apache' and the Ventures' 'Walk Don't Run' fail to carry the vital power of rock'n'roll the way 'Rumble' still does over twenty years later.

'What is love?/ Five feet of heaven in a pony-tail . . .' By the late 1950s the pop industry began turning out songs which had less grasp on reality than even the Everly Brothers' most romantic records. The revolt against the values of an older generation was gone. In its place came songs which dealt with the same teenage concerns but without any sense of toughness, threat or even real feeling. Wetness was the order of the day. If there was any doubt about it, one listen to Frankie Avalon's mawkish 'From Bobby Sox To Stockings' would prove the point:

> When a girl changes from bobby sox to stockings,
> And she starts trading her baby toys for boys,
> When that one shy little sleepyhead learns about
>   love and its lilt,
> You can bet that the change is more than from
>   cotton to silk . . .

Besides being a badly written song, all hint of sex is gone. Instead, an ideal young love was substituted with all the trappings of soda-pop and walking home from High School. It was 'Puppy Love' with 'Venus In Blue Jeans', 'Mona Lisa with a pony-tail'!

9 This rock'n'roll has got to go . . .

I reflect what's going on early enough to make a profit on it. I don't make culture. I sell it.

Dick Clark

The best rock'n'roll speaks with a personal voice direct to the listener. Rock'n'roll is a complete unit. The singer's personality, his style and his rebellious stance, the strength of the song, and the loudness and impact of the sound all go together to form the total effect. To take out one of those elements and hold it up for easy ridicule by people who have no feeling for that effect misses the point. So when Elvis said, 'I don't know anything about music – in my line I don't have to,' it isn't surprising that, though he knew he was right, the older generation laughed in scorn and took it as proof that rock'n'roll wasn't music at all but just an awful noise. They couldn't feel the all-important teenage social aspect or abandon themselves to that total experience. To them, music was polite, melodic and undemanding – if it wasn't, then it wasn't music.

In the best rock'n'roll there's clearly a sense of release, of exhilaration at breaking through musical and social conventions, of recording for the first time something wild and revolutionary, creative and fresher than tomorrow. When Elvis yells 'Hit it!' at the start of the guitar solo in 'Baby Let's Play House' you can hear that sort of excitement in his voice.

When the pop industry began trying to manufacture rock'n'roll, it failed because it was this spontaneity, excitement and total experience that it couldn't begin to capture. It could succeed only in producing some of the individual parts that made up rock'n'roll without ever managing to make the whole thing sound right. Rock'n'roll came from the performers, not the industry.

August 1957   Philadelphia policeman's son, fourteen-year-old Fabiano Forte, future hit singer of 'Tiger' and 'Turn Me Loose' is discovered.

> I was sitting on my front doorstep when a car pulled up, and the driver came over and said I looked a bit like Ricky Nelson. He asked if I could sing, and I told him sure, but mainly in the bath. He then introduced himself as Bob Marcucci, and asked if I'd ever thought of making a record. I said that I hadn't and he drove off, but he came back some weeks later with his partner Peter de Angelis, and I signed with them to record for the Chancellor record label.

Chancellor already had seventeen-year-old Frankie Avalon under contract and the records they made were the industry's idea of cleaned-up rock'n'roll. Sax solos lost their hard, exciting edge, electric guitars were buried in the comfortable, undemanding sound. It was attractive and you could dance to it, but the edgy, volcanic excitement of rock'n'roll was gone. In New York, Connie Francis sang the same sort of production-line rock'n'roll mixed with unrebellious teen appeal. This was pop music.

Top Forty radio played its part in their success. Alan Freed had pioneered an individual style for an

independent station. But soon the independent
stations were amalgamated into chains across the
country. The disc-jockey's freedom to play what he
liked was restricted by the introduction of a Top
Forty playlist. He was to programme each week only
forty chosen records. This is what Britain's Radio
One was doing in the 1970s, and has become the
basic structure of pop radio. To get radio play, record
companies would have to appeal to the widest
possible audience. And that meant playing it safe. No
more outrage and no more rock'n'roll? Well, not
quite, but the pressure was on. Part of it came from
Dick Clark's daily networked TV show *American
Bandstand.*

In the studio a teenage audience danced, held
hands and applauded the show's star guests as they
mimed to their latest records. An appearance on the
show boosted record sales. Even the regular
audience became celebrities, receiving fan mail and
questions about the romances they had with each
other off the set. Clark looked like your clean-cut,
moral, older brother and he appealed to adults too.
Record companies aimed their products straight at
American Bandstand. The whole thing was a
marketing device. The industry had discovered how
to turn rock'n'roll into big business and still keep
control. Other industries grew up around it as spin
offs: clothes styles as worn by the pop stars, picture
badges, or, as one commentator put it, 'If one bought
a picture of Frankie Avalon doing the Twist at
Malibu, the record was thrown in free.'

Payola   Disc-jockeys were in the best possible position to
give an extra plug to records in which they had a
financial interest. Clark had many such business
connections but said he never knowingly plugged a

record. None the less, record companies gave DJs gifts – a holiday perhaps, cash or a percentage of the royalties on a hit. It went beyond mere advertising. Much of it was bribery and the practice became known as Payola.

In 1960 the US Senate began an investigation. As a result, several DJs were convicted. Alan Freed was amongst them, but Dick Clark wasn't. Musically the Payola scandal confirmed the Philadelphia approach. Now only safe songs were released, all trace of aggressive rock'n'roll was removed. It was back to the early 1950s, only this time they used teenage singers, sometimes literally picking them up off the streets. In Stan Freberg's 'Payola Roll Blues', a record executive is cruising the streets in his limousine when he spots a likely-looking teenager:

> 'Hey kid!'
> 'Who, me?'
> 'Yeah, you – can you sing?'
> 'Nope.'
> 'Good, come with me . . . you got a pretty face and a pompadour – you got all the things you need to make a hit rock'n'roll record.'

In Philadelphia in the late 1950s there was more than a grain of truth in Freberg's song.

10 Shakin' all over: Britain in the late 1950s

> I hate rock'n'roll. It must be the only form of music
> which the majority of musicians who are playing it
> dislike too.
>
> Pete Murray

> Don'tcha touch me, baby
> 'Cos I'm shakin' so much!
>
> Johnny Kidd

There was no Payola scandal in Britain, but similar
business pressures were at work.

On the radio, the BBC, as always, held the
monopoly. It changed little. Apart from the Saturday
night Top Twenty show *Pick Of The Pops*, you
sometimes heard some rock'n'roll on Sunday
lunchtime on the request show *Two-Way Family
Favourites*. And that was it until October 1958 when
Saturday morning's *Skiffle Club* became two hours
of *Saturday Club*. There, compère Brian Matthew
introduced live sessions from the week's guests, a
spot of interviewing and new record releases.

Far and away the best bet, however, was to tune
in, evenings only, to 208 metres on the medium
waveband: Radio Luxembourg and its record-
company-sponsored shows.

Television and Jack Good

The Six-Five-Special's steaming down the line,
Six-Five-Special – right on time . . .

Television, however, was more open to new things, if only because, being new, all things were new to it. *Juke Box Jury* began in 1959. Compère David Jacobs played some of the week's new singles to a panel of celebrities who gave their opinion and voted the records a 'hit' or a 'miss'. Mostly they didn't like rock'n'roll.

Young BBC producer Jack Good was the man who did most for rock'n'roll on TV. At five past six on 16 February 1957, a steam train lurched into view on the nation's tiny TV screens and '6.5 Special' was on its way. It was a jolly, youth-clubby show featuring teenage performers in amongst comedians and ballad singers. It seemed genuinely innovative. 'It's the wonderful friendly spirit which exists both on and off the set,' said presenter Pete Murray, 'which is responsible for the informal effect.' If you watched the show now that informality would seem pretty forced. But, then, it was a startlingly free-and-easy programme.

Jack Good was the man responsible for that. He pioneered the intruding yet natural camerawork which pop generally needs. It didn't matter if things went wrong: if a mike-boom came into view, or an entire camera-crew could be seen filming away. It all matched the spirit of the music and Good succeeded in capturing it like no one else.

I had this idea of featuring a glomeration of kids between the camera and the artiste in an effort to capture the excitement of rock'n'roll. But this was completely new. Always the audience had been behind the camera, now I was trying to put them in front. It wouldn't work, the BBC told me. I was hauled up before the Head of Light Entertainment and ordered to behave.

Unknown to his superiors, Good had the studio set built on wheels.

As soon as the audience came in, I got the set swung round on the wheels so that the kids just had to be in the show. There was chaos. The band was blaring. The kids were jiving, and I was shouting at the top of my voice for more noise, more action. Then the chief walked in. He gazed dumbfounded at what was happening to his programme. Silence descended on the studio. I broke into a sweat. 'Carry on', he said, then beat a hasty retreat.

The BBC had competition from the new commercial station, ITV, which had begun in 1955. Soon ITV had Good producing the all pop and rock'n'roll show *Oh Boy!*, the best of the 1950s' TV shows. Television's rapid growth as family entertainment put pressure on would-be rock'n'roll singers to appeal to a family audience. Realising this, Good forced a professional approach onto his artists, especially Cliff Richard. His sideboards were cut, a suitable stage costume found and his wilder rock'n'roll movements toned down. In the long run a smile gets you a bigger audience than a scowl was the golden rule. Television boosted the careers of both Cliff and Marty Wilde. Their success came as rock'n'roll spread to a younger age-group – just too young to feel they had been in at the beginning.

Marty Wilde   All the people down the street
Whoever you meet
Say I'm a bad boy.

Success – Marty Wilde and a new set of white-walled wheels

'Bad Boy' is perhaps Marty's best record. His light moody voice became less distinctive as he went on, but on his best records he still sounds good. His first big hit was 'Endless Sleep'. His sullen, Presleyish good looks and the suicidal lyrics ('This is one that we can well do without,' said *NME*'s record reviewer!) made a convincing image. He appeared frequently on TV and compered Jack Good's follow-up show to *Oh Boy!*, a job which he performed well.

I'm hoping that the series will eventually help me to become a TV personality, instead of just a singer. You see, my aim is to become an all-round entertainer and via a show like *Boy Meets Girls* I hope to reach a wider audience.

He reached that wider audience, but he also fought against being backed on record by unsympathetic sessionmen. Eventually his own band, the Wildcats, recorded with him.

It was Cliff who finally outlasted Marty and dominated British pop until the arrival of the Beatles in 1963. In many ways Marty stood between the early attempts at cashing in on rock'n'roll and the complete taming of it into early 1960s' beat music. Cliff had a lot to do with that process.

Cliff Richard   *Summer 1958*   An agent watches Cliff and his group the Drifters (soon to become the Shadows) and finds them a summer season booking at Butlin's Holiday Camp, Clacton: free board and lodging and £9 a week each. A demo-disc is cut and sent to Columbia Records. They are impressed and record Cliff singing a cover of an American song 'Schoolboy Crush'.

It's the B-side of the record, however, which reaches the top of the charts, a song written by the Drifters' guitarist Ian Samwell, and called 'Move It'.

> Come on pretty baby, let's a-move it and a-groove it,
> Well shake oh baby shake oh honey please don't lose it,
> The rhythm that gets into your heart and soul,
> Let me tell you baby, it's called rock'n'roll.

Was it rock'n'roll? Well, yes, in a way it was. It wasn't rockabilly nor the screaming r'n'b of Little Richard. It was a British hybrid rock'n'roll: medium-paced, moodily sung, with a cleanly recorded guitar sound and a pulsating bass line in the style of Duane Eddy.

Cliff modelled himself on Elvis, and, like him, his stage movements provoked outraged comments

opposite
Cliff Richard the
rock'n'roller

from those who believed he was portraying sex on stage. They were probably right. But he lacked the toughness of Elvis. Nevertheless, his early rock'n'roll discs were better than most. The difference with Cliff was that he sounded more than halfway convincing – and that, in 1958–9 was more than enough.

over page, left
Neatness and
smiles in style –
Cliff and Hank
Marvin of the
Shadows

> They say it's gonna die, but honey, please let's
>   face it,
> Well we just don't know what's going to replace it.

'Living Doll' replaced it. Cliff thought it wasn't really rock'n'roll. He was right, but when asked to sing it as a jog-along almost-country ballad, he reluctantly agreed. It brought him a family audience. Teenage music with a family appeal triumphed in the summer of 1959 – rock'n'roll went underground. Cliff was more than just firmly in the mainstream of pop and showbusiness. He was becoming the mainstream. His success was the one that British managers and promoters now tried to copy. Raw rock'n'roll was a greasy, Brylcreemed embarrassment – and suspiciously working class and uninhibited too. The entertainment business was happier with the sort of well-groomed singers it could turn into teenage versions of the Dickie Valentines and Lita Rozas of yesteryear. Billy Fury though was different.

Billy Fury

When he was in his middle teens, he wanted to wear drainpipe jeans but his father wouldn't let him. So he'd sneak out of the house into the back yard and hide his drainpipes in the outdoor lavatory. Then, when the time came to go out, he'd saunter away all innocent in his baggy flannels, whip round the corner, up over the back lane wall, rescue his drainpipes from the can and finally hit town in full splendour. That was determination.

over page, right
Billy Fury

That was his exact difference – could anyone imagine Tommy Steele or Terry Dene going to all that trouble just to be an image rocker?

Nik Cohn

Billy grew up in one of the tougher parts of Liverpool. When he left school he worked on the River Mersey tugboats. In the autumn of 1958 Marty Wilde came to the Birkenhead Essoldo.

That night Billy caught the ferry across the Mersey and managed to get backstage before the show. He persuaded Marty to listen to some of his songs. Marty and his manager were impressed with Billy as well as the songs. Before he knew what was happening, he was opening the show that night armed with a guitar and the songs he'd previously sung only to himself at home.

It was a classic success story. Billy went down a storm and was sent home to pack a suitcase for the rest of the tour. It's his early records on which his rock'n'roll reputation rests. Although, like everybody else, he tried to sing in the breathy, moody Elvis way, he had too much of a feeling for rock'n'roll to be confined to that. Many of his songs show how well he understood the music and could write it himself.

In the end, urged by his father, Billy announced that he would 'clean up' his act. He held out longer than most and, at the turn of the 1950s, managed to come closer than any of his predecessors to the essence of rock'n'roll.

Interlude   *Spring 1958*   Jerry Lee Lewis arrived in London for a tour. Newspapers splashed across their front pages news of his recent marriage. It wasn't just that it was his third – but that his new wife was his cousin

and she was *only thirteen* . . . ! The truth was that
Myra was a far-removed third cousin, and as for her
age? Well, there was nothing illegal about marrying
so young in the southern rural communities they both
came from.

'We have more than enough rock'n'roll
entertainers of our own without importing them from
overseas,' said an MP in the House of Commons.

Jerry was unimpressed: 'I don't give a damn about
it. I wanted to get married. I got married. They don't
like it, they can kiss my butt.'

Portrayed by the Press as a cradle-snatcher, he
stormed ahead with his tour. His real fans stood by
him – if anything, his status with them grew because
of all the fuss – but the rest of his audience hurled
abuse and the tour ground to a halt. Unrepentant,
Jerry and Myra went home leaving the British Press
congratulating itself on its moral victory.

By the end of the 1950s there were three
American rock'n'rollers who found a special status in
Britain. Buddy Holly and the Crickets toured in
March 1958, and the power of their music live was a
revelation to British audiences. But two of the most
well-loved rock'n'rollers in Britain were Gene Vincent
and Eddie Cochran.

Gene Vincent and Eddie Cochran in Britain

Say mama can I go out tonight?
Say mama will it be alright?
They got a rockin' party goin' down the street,
Say mama can't you hear that beat? . . .

Gene Vincent

December 1959   Gene Vincent arrives at London
Airport. He isn't like the pretty, inoffensive pop
singers who are replacing rock'n'roll: his greasy,
working-class image is all wrong, he is too obviously

a rock'n'roll singer – a wild man. Jack Good is at
the airport. To his surprise the man he meets is not a
mean, vicious, guitar-wielding hoodlum but a polite,
soft-spoken young man who, like Elvis, calls
everyone 'Sir' or 'Ma'am'.

Claiming Shakespeare's Richard III and Hamlet as
his models, Good moulded Gene into the image that
became the most potent in all rock'n'roll. He dressed
him entirely in black leather, with gloves to match,
and hung around his neck a huge silver medallion.

'Limp, you bugger, limp!' Good is supposed to
have hissed at him across the TV studio in an
attempt to exploit Gene's injured leg. His tour was a
tremendous success – like Jerry Lee, Gene on stage
was the epitome of rock'n'roll.

> The curtain would go up and Gene would be there
> like some demon possessed by the beat, face
> contorted in an agonised smile and his huge eyes
> staring at some vision only he could see. He'd lean
> on the mike-stand like some drunk trying to
> support himself. Suddenly, he'd swing his left leg
> right over the mike, spin round 360 degrees and
> tear into the first number. Transformed into a
> crouching wildcat, he'd carry the mikestand a few
> feet off the ground, spin, throw, and catch it in a
> single short burst of movement. Then he'd be
> stock still for minutes on end.

Eddie Cochran followed Gene to Britain. British
rock'n'roll fans couldn't believe it. Polite pop music
seemed to have buried rock'n'roll. Yet, here it was,
in April 1960 – Duane Eddy had toured the previous
month and now here were two of the original
rock'n'rollers.

Looking back, far from being a new beginning, it
turned out to be the final act. The last date of the

tour was the Bristol Hippodrome. After the show,
Gene, Eddie and his fiancée climbed in the back of
a taxi for London Airport and home for a short rest.
They were due to return for a long summer tour. It's
said that, after not having played any of Buddy
Holly's records since Buddy's death, Eddie put some
on the record player the night before the taxi-ride.

In the early hours of Sunday morning, on the A4
outside Chippenham, the car burst a tyre, swerved
across the road and hit a lamp-post. The others in
the car were only injured, but Eddie was thrown up
into the car roof. Later that morning he died of
severe head injuries. It was 17 April 1960. A few
weeks later his ironically titled 'Three Steps To
Heaven' reached Number One to give him his
biggest-ever hit.

> Skinny white sailor, the chances were slender,
> The beauties were brief.
> Shall I mourn your decline with some Thunderbird
>   wine
> And a black handkerchief –
> I miss your sad, Virginia whisper,
> I miss the voice that caught my heart.
>
> Ian Dury, 'Sweet Gene Vincent'

Gene's injuries made his already damaged leg
worse. This, his life on the road and associated
drinking problems all contributed to his early death in
1971. For several years he lived and worked in
Britain. Often his shows couldn't have been better,
sometimes they were embarrassing. The life he led
and the knocks he received took their toll and it
showed. The bad performances shed light on the
man but leave the legend intact. In the audience at
one of Eddie and Gene's last shows together was
disc-jockey John Peel:

I first heard Gene Vincent when I was at school and was amazed by his voice and the incredible country rock music of the Bluecaps. His high whining voice I still believe to be the most impressive to come out of rock'n'roll . . . I converted the whole of my troop in the Royal Artillery to their music and the concert we all attended at the Liverpool Empire with Gene and the late Eddie Cochran was something I'll never forget.

But if Eddie's death was the final act, then the man who wrote the postscript and linked the rock'n'roll era with the 1960s was Johnny Kidd.

Shakin' all over: Johnny Kidd and the Pirates

The summer of 1959 was teenage love-song time. 'Donna', 'Teenager In Love', 'Only Sixteen', 'Dream Lover', 'Lonely Boy' – you hardly need to hear them to know what they were about!

But I remember that summer for two rock'n'roll records that stuck in my mind on first hearing and have remained there ever since. One was Ronnie Hawkins's 'Forty Days'. But the other accompanied me wherever I went. It was Johnny Kidd's 'Please Don't Touch'. So well did I know it that I could play it in my mind whenever I wished – in fact, it played itself for most of the time whether I liked it or not!

Well I don't know why she's got her claws in me,
I wanna be a bachelor and fancy-free
Runnin' from the preacher, boy! what a relief!
I'm gonna spend my life shakin' like a leaf
Well I remember well the first time her ruby lips
    brushed my cheek
I opened up my mouth but the rest of me just
    wouldn't speak
Ple-ease don't touch – I shake so much . . .

So many words crammed into such a short song, driven by one of the most powerful guitar and drum backings I'd heard. It was excellent rock'n'roll – and it was British.

The really big hit, however, came a year later: the summer of 1960, which to some meant the Shadows' 'Apache' at Number One. To others it was the summer of 'Shakin' All Over'. Where the Shadows were restrained and polite, Johnny Kidd and the Pirates were tense and menacing. 'Apache' was pop music – 'Shakin' All Over' was rock'n'roll.

Johnny came from north London, and graduated from skiffle to his own band, writing a lot of his own songs. On stage, to augment the pirate image, he wore a black eye-patch and the band dressed in pirate clothes complete with cutlasses.

Johnny eventually replaced the original Pirates with the band that came together again in the mid-1970s: Frank Farley on drums, Johnny Spence on bass and Mick Green on lead guitar. If 'Please Don't Touch' and 'Shakin' All Over' were rock'n'roll hits out of their time, the new band moved quickly ahead of everyone else. They recorded some r'n'b which at that time, the early 1960s, was refreshing and exciting. The band worked hard on one-night stands too, playing in dance-halls and, like other rock bands short of bookings, at the Star Club in Hamburg.

In the doldrums again after another bout of success in the wake of the Beatles, but still recording and touring, Johnny was killed in a car crash in October 1966.

There were touches of Gene Vincent in Johnny's singing, but he didn't sound like a carbon-copy of the American rock'n'rollers. It was his own British voice that distinctively came through – in that, too, he was ahead of his time.

And finally? Well, Johnny said in 1960 'Maybe you
think it's strange that I should ever have written a
piece called "Shakin' All Over" . . . Titles like this,
they say, went out in the very early days of
rock'n'roll.' He was right. Titles like that *had*
disappeared. But in the end 'Shakin' All Over' is
perhaps the only British rock'n'roll disc that can hold
its own with the great American originals.

11 It doesn't matter any more

I can't stand that surfing shit. Rock'n'roll's been
going downhill ever since Buddy Holly died.

From the film *American Graffitti*

And so, by 1960, it seemed to be all over. What had
happened?

Rock'n'roll's vitality and freshness had been
sapped by show business and the established record
industry. As early as 1957, new young singers were
doing what would safely make money inside show
business rather than reacting against it and doing
what they felt was right. Even Elvis, on his return
from the Army, seemed to have thrown in the towel
and turned to the semi-operatic pop of 'It's Now Or
Never'. It was his biggest-selling world-wide hit since
1956. He *was* a pop singer now. And in Britain,
many of those who'd been inspired by him were
already pop singers, not rock'n'rollers.

In America, some of the original rock'n'rollers
themselves had returned either to country music or
rhythm'n'blues – though the styles they turned to
were heavily influenced by rock'n'roll and the
demands of a large pop audience.

Carl Perkins's music was mostly overlooked;
Johnny Burnette was writing and successfully
recording pop songs. Already by 1957 Ronnie

Hawkins was on his way north to find work in Canada, and to form a group which, in the 1960s, without him, would join Bob Dylan and become known as the Band.

But the fates of some others were very different.

Little Richard had renounced rock'n'roll and turned his considerable energy and talent to the church.

In different ways, Jerry Lee Lewis and Gene Vincent had both been discredited. Jerry Lee survived the outcry over his marriage, but the mud thrown at him still stuck. Gene Vincent's working-class image was against him in the States, but in Britain he was still a hero.

Chuck Berry was facing criminal charges for transporting a girl, who was legally under-age, over a state-line. The prosecution claimed his motives to be 'immoral purposes'. He was found guilty and sentenced to two years in prison.

Eddie Cochran was dead.

And so was Buddy Holly. Early in 1959 he'd set out on a tour of the mid-west. The organisation wasn't all it might have been and Buddy was tired when the package show played the Surf Ballroom, Clear Lake, Iowa. Rather than spend yet another night crammed into a bus for the three hundred miles to the next show, he chartered a plane to take him on ahead. Two other singers, Ritchie Valens and The Big Bopper joined him. Towards one in the morning of 3 February they took off in a small Beechcraft Bonanza heading for Fargo in north Dakota. It was snowing and the pilot had to rely on his instruments. No one knows exactly what happened next. At daylight the wreckage of the plane was found a few miles away piled up in the snow against a fence. All the occupants were dead.

As Don Maclean sang in his big hit 'American Pie'

Daily Mirror — Tragedy of 'Jape' Richardson

THEY CALLED HIM—

BIG BOPPER

FEB 4 1959

2½ FORWARD WITH THE PEOPLE
No. 17,150

TOP 'ROCK' STARS DIE IN CRASH

From BARRIE HARDING, New York, Tuesday

THREE of America's top rock 'n' roll stars were killed in a plane crash today, a few hours after delighting teenagers at a "big beat" concert.

They were BUDDY HOLLY, whose recording of "That'll Be The Day" sold more than a million and a half copies; BIG BOPPER (Jape Richardson), singer of the current hit "Chantilly Lace"; and RITCHIE VALENS, composer of the Tommy Steele favourite "Come On, Let's Go."

All three appeared last night at a winter ball for teenagers at Lake North, Iowa. Early this morning they

boarded a small charter plane at Mason City to fly to Fargo, North Dakota, where they were billed to appear tonight.

The plane took off in a slight snowstorm — and nothing more was heard of it.

Hours later the pilot of a search plane spotted wreckage on a farm about ten miles from Mason City.

The bodies of the three stars and the pilot, Roger Perterson, lay near by.

Bad weather is blamed for the crash.

On TV Here

BUDDY HOLLY, 22, was married only seven months ago.

He was the star of the group called "The Crickets" and shot to the top of the hit parade with records like "That'll Be The Day" and "Peggy Sue."

Buddy visited Britain last March and was seen by

millions of viewers in a Sunday Night at the London Palladium show.

His latest record — called "It Doesn't Matter Any More" — has not been released.

BIG BOPPER was a disc jockey and had appeared in minstrel shows where he created the Big Bopper character.

And that was the name he adopted for his first record "Chantilly Lace" which he a so composed on film on British TV recently.

Last week "Chantilly Lace" was No. 12 in the Mirror's Pop Twenty.

RITCHIE VALENS gave his age as twenty-one.

But the Hollywood company dealing with his records said tonight that in fact he was only seventeen.

He left school on his last year.

Buddy Holly ... as Britain saw him.

7 days FREE Viewing

D.E.R. 21st ANNIVERSARY OFFER

... only 7'6 a week

POST NOW ▶

D·E·R

600,000 JOBLESS?

By ROLAND HURMAN
Mirror Industrial Editor

TOP trade union leaders are convinced that the total number of unemployed people in Britain is now more than 600,000. Some of them fear the figure may be as high as 620,000.

Official unemployment figures are

due to be published next week by the Ministry of Labour.

The last census of unemployed was taken on January 12 and the job of consolidating the returns from all the employment exchanges has taken longer than usual.

THE NEW FIGURES ARE EXPECTED TO SHOW THE MOST ALARMING INCREASE OF JOBLESS OVER A ONE-MONTH PERIOD FOR MANY YEARS

In December the total was 537,600.

Mr. Iain Macleod, Minister of Labour, has already revealed in Parliament, answers steep rises of unemployment in certain areas in Scotland and the North.

If the new total has reached 672,000 it would be roughly 2.8 per cent of the working population the proportion forecast by Mr. Macleod in Commons last November as a possible figure for Britain's recession.

---

3 February 1959
– the day the
music died?

several years later, to many people that cold February day in 1959 was 'the day the music died'.

And Alan Freed? The man whose radio programme had introduced a young white audience to rhythm'n'blues? In the Payola trials he was fined

and given a suspended sentence. Early in 1965,
while awaiting trial on new charges of evading
income tax, he died in hospital aged only forty-three.

Some folks don't understand it,
That's why they don't demand it, . . .
It'll be here for ever and ever,
Ain't gonna fade, never no never,
It's swept this whole wide land,
Rock'n'roll forever will stand.

The Showmen

12 Rock'n'roll is here to stay

There is no power on earth that can stop an idea whose time has come.

I remember coming out of the Elephant and Castle, the big theatre at the corner – the Trocadero – and it was after seeing the Bill Haley film *Rock Around The Clock*, and we all went down the Old Kent Road, and at the end of the Old Kent Road, all the fire engines were there, and they got their hoses all ready, and it was a big thing, terrible big thing. You felt you were it. Not only just because you were young, but you felt the rest of your lives would be, well, ordered by you and not ordered by other people. We thought we could do anything we bloody well wanted – we thought we could do anything at all – nothing could stop you. You were the guv'nor – you were the king. The world was free – the world was open.

Ray Gosling

Society was already changing by the time rock'n'roll arrived. The music defined those changes as they related to young people and created a teenage culture for the first time.

Society was forced to look more closely at teenage lifestyles. Youth now had an increasing economic power. When Mark Abrams produced his report on 'The Teenage Consumer' he noted that the total expenditure of single young people in 1960 was a staggering £900 million. He was officially stating what had been obvious to manufacturers since the mid-1950s: that there was a huge new teenage market to produce goods for and make profits from.

British Prime Minister Harold Macmillan said in 1957:

> Indeed let us be frank about it: most of our people have never had it so good. Go round the country, go to the industrial towns, go to the farms, and you will see a state of prosperity such as we have never had in my lifetime – nor indeed ever in the history of this country.

In this world young people felt increasingly independent. Rock'n'roll sang of this independence, gloried in it, and reflected it back in its powerful sound, its lyrics and, most of all, in the rebellious stand it seemed to take against adult and establishment values. Rock'n'roll was this new freedom. This new brash, confident music was made by young people for young people. At least for the time being youth was calling the tune.

The boundaries of this new world were defined by sometimes hysterical adult criticism. If parents, teachers, politicians and the establishment in all its forms from the Press to the church to the magistrates' courts to the House of Lords said how much they hated rock'n'roll, then it must be all right.

Attitudes towards the music marked off the generations more radically than anything else. Adults didn't understand how on earth young people could possibly like rock'n'roll, dressing up like Teddy boys and juvenile delinquents, wearing their hair long and greased, staying out late in pubs and coffee bars, and enjoying themselves in such a rude, inconsiderate, anti-social way. 'They've got more money and a better education than we ever had,' they complained. 'Why are they so ungrateful?' It was rightly seen as a rebellion against out-dated ideas which had little to do with the new post-war world which the Teddy boys jiving in the aisles to Bill Haley felt they were part of. The excitement of rock'n'roll and the joyous optimism of living for the moment were no part of an older society still carefully clinging to pre-war attitudes.

Although there was more money, however, there were few amenities provided for young people. There was greater educational opportunity but this was of little benefit if you were leaving school at fifteen to the threat of National Service. Significantly rock'n'roll appealed first, especially in Britain, to working-class youth. It was the Teddy boys who were rock'n'roll's first audience. And by the early 1960s it was the largely working-class rockers, with their leather jackets and powerful Norton motorbikes, who kept allegiance to the rock'n'rollers. It was they who filled transport 'caffs' like the legendary Ace on the North Circular Road, playing sometimes fatal games: the favourite was putting a record on the jukebox and riding a motorbike over a mile to the roundabout to be back inside the cafe before the record ended.

But rock'n'roll didn't appeal to everyone under the age of twenty. Some sections of middle-class youth preferred folk and folk-blues. In America they turned to the Kingston Trio and the early Bob Dylan, in ways which are discussed more fully in Brian Carroll's *Contemporary Folk Music*. In Britain they clung to the more authentic aspects of skiffle, and later crowded out the trad-jazz clubs wearing a beatnik-style uniform of sloppy sweaters, jeans and duffle-coats, many becoming supporters of the Campaign for Nuclear Disarmament.

Between these two groups was the majority. Younger than the Teddy boys and perhaps not as politically aware as those who joined the CND, they too were caught up in the tremendous youth explosion created by rock'n'roll. Instead of following adult notions of good taste in clothes young people began choosing things that weren't 'sensible' or 'made to last' – which usually meant dull and boring. By the mid-1950s, jeans, T-shirts and sneakers were fairly common in the United States, but blue denim jeans began appearing in Britain only as rock'n'roll got under way. Generally, clothes became more attractive, emphasising the lines of the body rather than hiding them as the baggy suits of the older generation had done.

The Italian style, with its narrow trousers and shoulders and shorter 'bum-freezer' jackets, arrived in the late 1950s. But often existing fashions were altered to fit a faster, more streamlined style of living. Shirt collars were turned up at the back; ties became narrower ('slim-jims'). Socks, made of synthetic fibres, not wool, came in garish, sometimes striped colours, and were worn ankle-length. Shoes were at first of the 'mudguard' variety, and then thick crepe-soled, perhaps brogue or suede – it was only later that long pointed-toe 'winkle-pickers' arrived. Trousers were tighter fitting and narrowed to the ankle, occasionally even needing a zip to make getting the foot in and out easier. Great importance was attached to what was worn and how. Style, flash and stance meant everything: a schoolfriend became the envy of the class on announcing that he'd persuaded his mother to taper even his pyjama trousers to twelve-inch bottoms!

In the end, just as rock'n'roll's early revolt became tamed, so too did the more extreme elements of the wider youth explosion. Attitudes and even clothes and hairstyles were dramatically toned down by the start of the 1960s. It was as if rock'n'roll was the first battle in what was often referred to as a war between the generations. But that battle made only a temporary breach in the barricades and a quick retreat by the older generation to new and better-defended positions. Rock'n'roll came from the generation born just before or during the Second World War. The next assault would be carried out by their successors who had grown up to rock'n'roll itself.

Without Elvis, rock'n'roll might have been just another musical style. But it was more than that. Without the changes in society that were going on, without the impatient wish for freedom felt by the teenage generation of the 1950s, Elvis himself might have been just a rock'n'roll singer. As it was, he and the ferocious, physical blast of raw rock'n'roll made the past suddenly appear as dead as it really was. It was a complete break, clearing the decks for a new future in which young people and new ideas had a part to play.

None of this could have been foreseen by Sam Phillips or Alan Freed, but they sensed that something was going on that was not just a shift in musical tastes. Rock'n'roll sprang directly from the young audience that felt society's changes most keenly. Because it was close to its listeners and mirrored their lives, rock'n'roll remained fresh, assertive and vital.

Memphis, Tenn.
Elvis Presley, the Mississippi boy whose country

rock guitar and gyrating hips launched a new style in popular music, died Tuesday afternoon at Baptist Hospital, police said. He was 42.

Associated Press bulletin, 16 August 1977

Elvis is dead now. He died at a time when another pop explosion was taking place as the music and attitudes of the Sex Pistols and punk rock exploded against the blandness and lack of contact with young people of the industry-dominated pop music of the 1970s. He died, too, at a time when, in Britain, rockabilly – that first white southern rock'n'roll – had never been so popular. Despite America's cold-shouldering of rock'n'roll as the 1950s ended, groups of British listeners kept the music alive in record-collecting, small magazines, societies and fan-clubs, dedicated partly to researching the music and its origins. Often the feelings were very one-sided:

> Some of the people who appeared in the R'n'R Top 20s were not, are not, and *never will be* classed as Rock'n'Roll . . . names like Conman Twitty, Marty Tame, Rickety Nelson and several others. Why, we even got great rockin' cats like Johnny 'Cry' Ray, Bob 'Junkie' Dylan and that great bopping (?) twosome, Simon and Garbage-uncle! . . . But I can assure all the true Bop-Cats in the Club who *really* dig R'n'R that these names will *never* appear on the pages of 'Rock'n'Roll News', at least not in any serious article! Some may say that we are too purist, but nobody asks to see articles in *Downbeat* [a jazz magazine] on Acker Bilk or Kenny Ball . . . Well, now I've got that little lot off my chest, I'll get on with the job in hand . . . writing about *the*, my music, *your* kind of music . . .

Rock'n'Roll
Read on, cats, hope you dig,
Yours be-bop-a-shakingly,
Rockin' Robin.

From this base in the 1970s came a revival of interest in Elvis's original music. There is a new audience which wasn't even born when Elvis, Scotty and Bill were recording in Memphis. To them, too, a quarter of a century later, rock'n'roll and a music they can take part in and make themselves holds more power and meaning than anything the pop industry might manufacture for them.

'Rock'n'roll is simply an attitude,' said Johnny Thunders of the Heartbreakers in 1977. 'You don't have to play the greatest guitar.' The Heartbreakers didn't play 1950s' rock'n'roll, but its spirit was at the heart of their music, performance and lifestyle. 'Hail, hail, rock'n'roll,' sang Chuck Berry in 1956, 'deliver us from the days of old.'

It did.

Anyone who says rock'n'roll is a passing fad or a flash-in-the-pan trend along the music road has *rocks in the head*, dad!

Alan Freed

Glossary of musical terms

Afro-American music   Any music which combines African and European elements. Such music was first made by black people in America, but the term can now be applied to any music in the style.

Arrangement   An arrangement is a new version of an existing piece of music (unlike a *composition*, which is a completely new piece of music).

backbeat drumming   Drumming in which the *backbeat* (also called the *offbeat*) is strongly stressed (i.e., one TWO three FOUR). This sound is very typical of r'n'b and rock'n'roll.

ballad   This word has several meanings. In this book it means: A short sentimental popular song, usually fairly slow in speed, of the sort produced by Tin Pan Alley. (This is the sense meant in connection with the song 'Blue Moon' on p. 24.)

bass   The lowest pitched part of a piece of music. *String bass (double bass)*: a stringed instrument used for playing bass parts, in appearance like a large, upright violin.

Bluegrass   A form of **country and western music** created originally by Bill Monroe. (For details see pp. 23–24.)

cajun   A type of white music, strongly influenced by black music, and found in Louisiana. It often features the accordion.

call-and-response form   A method of music making in which a leader (possibly improvising) sings a line (the *call*), and is answered by a chorus (the *response*). The *call* and *response* are usually one line long each. This procedure is an important feature of all Afro-American music.

chord   The result of sounding three or more notes together. It is an important function of the piano and guitar to play chords.

country and western music   The music which was most popular with white people in the southern states of the USA after about 1920.

folk music   The popular music of one community. In practice, the music of rural societies of the past. Folk music was usually sung, and was passed on by ear. In this book the folk music mentioned is white American music of the eastern USA, which is derived from older British folk music. (For further details see *Folksong and Music Hall*, pp. 34–7.)

gospel music   Black American religious music performed in concert conditions by touring performers (as distinct from the spontaneous music of black American religious services).

harmony   (1) The 'harmony (or harmonies) of a tune' are the **chords** which accompany it. (2) When musicians study harmony, they study the *rules governing the use of chords*. (3) To 'harmonise' a tune is to fit harmonies to it.

hoedown   A name for an American rural social gathering featuring square dancing.

improvisation   This word has several meanings. In this book it means: (1) The act of composing music at the moment of performance, rather than planning it beforehand. (2) Music in which the artist has planned the basic structure of a piece, but leaves some important aspects of expression, rhythm, etc., until the moment of performance. (In rock'n'roll singers and rhythm players improvise in this sense.) (3) On-the-spot composition of new lines of music, or very free versions of the melody. Such improvisation takes place over a set *chord progression*. (In rock'n'roll, a guitarist or saxist taking a solo, as in the music of Bill Haley, is improvising in this sense.)

New Orleans jazz   The jazz produced in New Orleans (Louisiana, USA) between about 1910 and 1930, or jazz in that style.

jazz   A form of Afro-American music which existed after about 1900, originally produced by black musicians, but later of international popularity. It was mostly *improvised* instrumental music. It was at first a form of dance music, but later developed into music for attentive listening.

Latin-American music   Music from Central and South America, and especially from Cuba and Brazil.

Latin-American percussion   Percussion instruments are ones which produce sound by being struck. In rock'n'roll the drums and cymbals are especially important members of this group of instruments. **Latin American music** is built over a percussion backing, and uses a special range of percussion instruments, of which the most important and well known are the maraccas and the claves.

lick   Any regularly used **phrase** in an Afro-American style, which is learned by instrumentalists for use in **improvisation**.

lyric   The words of a song.

mambo   A Latin-American dance in four-beat time, which became popular in the USA and Europe in the 1950s.

metaphor   This is a word with a range of often complicated meanings. In this book it means a technique of writing poetry and lyrics by which the writer appears to speak about one topic but is in fact referring to another.

music hall   A place of entertainment with mostly working-class audiences, popular in Britain between about 1820 and 1920. The performance would include singers, comedians and other variety artists, such as magicians and jugglers. (Though the popularity of the music hall declined rapidly after the First World War, it did not really die out until about 1960.)

pizzicato strings   The production of sound from stringed instruments such as the violin by plucking, rather than with a bow, as is normal.

phrase   Several notes which make up a very short tune. A single melodic idea.

phrasing   The interpretation of a **phrase** (by playing louder/softer, shorter/longer, smoother/rougher, etc.) to give it expressiveness and meaning.

popular music   Any music which is liked by a very large number of people (a mass audience). Usually, but not always, the musical taste of the majority. Popular music is also often defined, in contrast to classical music, as music for which a special training is not needed. This is not strictly correct, but it is true to say that popular music is music which is not normally studied in the music education system (e.g. at music colleges).

pop music   The music favoured by young people (under

25) since about 1955. The term includes rock'n'roll, reggae, Tamla Motown, etc.

quickstep   A twentieth-century ballroom dance in a quick four-beat time, in which couples hold each other close, and the man leads in performing intricate steps.

race music   The name given from about 1925 to 1950 to recordings by black artists and intended for a black American audience.

reverberation   Originally this word referred to the effect of strongly vibrating and echoing sound. In this book it refers to a special device in an amplification system, which makes an instrument sound as if it was being played in a large room.

riff   A musical technique which consists of the repetition of a particular **phrase**. It is often used to build up excitement, and for this reason was adopted by r'n'b bands.

rhythm'n'blues   (Also known as r'n'b.) The popular music of urban black Americans from about 1940 to 1960, and derived from the blues. (For details see pp. 30–7, and *Jazz and Blues*, pp. 116–24.)

royalties   Fees payable by a performer, or by the organisations which put on entertainment, for the right to use a copyright artistic work.

session man   A musician who, because of his very high competence in traditional techniques, including the reading of music, is hired for recording sessions (e.g. for film music, television commercials, and backings for singers).

sock rhythm   A punchy **country and western** rhythm created by hitting the **bass** and the guitar **chords** hard. (For details see p. 25.)

square dance   A form of country dance popular in the eastern areas of the United States. Such dances are derived from British folk dances. The dancers dance in square sets, and are guided by a caller.

swing   (1) The rhythmic effect obtained by jazz bands between about 1915 and 1965, or by bands after that date playing in an older style. (2) The rhythmic effect obtained by bands which, though not jazz bands, were influenced by jazz (for example, country and western and r'n'b bands). (3) 'Swing' (with capital S) is the name given to big band jazz and popular music, which enjoyed its greatest popularity in the 1930s and early 1940s.

thirds (See p. 92.) Often, when the Everly Brothers sang together, they did not both sing the tune. Instead, one of them sang the tune, and the other sang the same words in the same rhythm, but using different notes. Very often, when doing this they sang in *thirds*. Perhaps the easiest way to understand what this sounds like is to play one note on the piano keyboard (e.g. C, see diagram). Then at the same time play the *third* note from the left (i.e. E). You can then try doing the same with other notes (e.g. notes D and F, E and G, etc.).

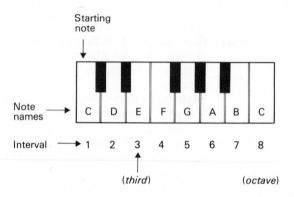

tone This word has several meanings. Strictly speaking, the word should be used to refer to the quality and character of sound made by *an individual performer*. However, the word is often used instead of *timbre*, which refers to the quality or character of sound made by a *particular instrument*, for example, the timbre (sound) of a violin, as compared to the timbre (sound) of a trumpet.

tremolo An effect used by electric instruments, and especially the guitar, in which the note seems to vibrate or tremble. It was especially popular in country and western and early British 'beat music'.

uptempo At a quick speed.

western swing A type of country music which became popular in the 1930s and 1940s. It took ideas from a variety of sources, including **jazz** and **swing**. (For details see pp. 23–4.)

Sources and acknowledgments

Songs 'Dear Hearts And Gentle People' (p. 1) written R. Hilliard, S. Fain (published E. H. Morris); 'Bell Bottom Boogie' (p. 2) written Moore, Ross and Stokes (Ardmore & Beechwood); the lines on p. 23 are from 'Time Changes Everything' written Tommy Duncan (Southern Music); 'Honky Tonk Blues' (p. 24) written Hank Williams (Robbins Music); 'Hillbilly Fever' (p. 25) written George Vaughn (Cherio Corp. N.Y.); 'Mind Your Own Business' and 'I'm So Lonesome I Could Cry' (p. 27) written H. Williams (Acuff-Rose); 'Good Rockin' Tonight' (p. 33) written Roy Brown (Ascherberg, Hopwood & Crew); 'Sixty Minute Man' (p. 33) written William Ward and Rose Marks (Fort Knox Music); 'Boppin' The Blues' (p. 45) and 'Dixie Fried' (p. 50) written C. Perkins, H. Griffin (Carlin Music Corp.); 'Riot In Cell Block No. 9' and 'Young Blood' (p. 66), 'That Is Rock'n'Roll' (p. 94) and the Coasters' 'Yakety Yak' (p. 99) written Jerry Leiber and Mike Stoller (Carlin Music Corp.); 'Hound Dog' (p. 46) written J. Leiber and M. Stoller (Chappell); 'Blue Suede Shoes' (p. 48) written C. Perkins (Carlin Music Corp.); 'High School Confidential' (p. 53) written Jerry Lee Lewis and Ron Hargrave (Carlin Music Corp.); 'Great Balls of Fire' (p. 53) written Jack Hammer and Otis Blackwell (Carlin Music Corp.); 'Roll Over Beethoven' (epigraph and p. 58), 'Johnny B. Goode' (p. 64), 'School Day' (pp. 96 and 97), 'Little Queenie' and 'Come On' (p. 98), 'Too Much Monkey Business' and 'Rock And Roll Music' (p. 98) written Chuck Berry (Jewel Music); 'Maybellene' (p. 58) written C. Berry, R. Fratto and A. Freed (Jewel Music); 'You Can't Catch Me' (p. 60) and 'Back In The USA' (p. 60) written Chuck Berry (Tristan Music); 'Tutti Frutti' (p. 61) written Richard Penniman and Dorothy La Bostrie (Burlington Music); 'Puttin' On The Style' (p. 73) written Cazden

(Essex Music); 'Rock Island Line' (p. 74) written L. Donegan (Essex Music); 'Twenty Flight Rock' (p. 77) written L. Fairchild and E. Cochran (Campbell Connolly); 'That'll Be The Day' (p. 86) written Jerry Allison, Buddy Holly and Norman Petty (Southern Music); 'Summertime Blues' (p. 88) written Eddie Cochran and Jerry Capehart (Cinephonic); 'C'mon Everybody' (pp. 88 and 98) written E. Cochran, J. Capehart (Burlington Music); 'Somethin' Else' (pp. 89 and 91) written E. Cochran and Sharon Sheeley (Burlington Music); 'Love And Marriage' (p. 94) written Sammy Cahn and Jimmy Van Heusen (Barton Music); 'Shake Rattle And Roll' (p. 94) written Charles Calhoun (Campbell Connolly); 'Long Tall Sally' (p. 95) written E. Johnson, R. Penniman and R. Blackwell (Southern Music); 'Wake Up Little Suzie' (p. 96) written Boudleaux and Felice Bryant (Acuff-Rose); 'Wear My Ring' (p. 97) written B. Carroll, R. Moody and M. Schack (Carlin Music Corp.); 'Stood Up' (p. 97) written D. Dickerson, E. Herrold (Francis, Day and Hunter); 'Route 66' (p. 98) written Bobby Troup (E. H. Morris & Co. Ltd.); Elvis's 'Party' (p. 98) written Robinson (Belinda Ltd); 'Weekend' (p. 99) written B. Post and D. Post (Cross Music); 'From Bobby Sox To Stockings' (p. 101) written Faith and Di Cicco (Debmar Publishing); the Playmates' 'What Is Love?' (p. 101) written P. Vance and L. Pockriss (Planetary-Kahl, London, Ltd); 'Payola Roll Blues' (p. 106) written S. Freberg (Freberg Music); 'Please Don't Touch' (pp. 107 and 120) written F. Heath and G. Robinson (Multimood Music); 'Six-Five Special' (p. 108) written Reine and More (Southern Music); 'Bad Boy' (p. 109) written Marty Wilde (Younstar Music); 'Move It' (p. 111) written Ian Samwell (Multimood Music); 'Say Mama' (p. 117) written J. Meeks and J. Earl (Peter Maurice); 'Sweet Gene Vincent' (p. 119) written Ian Dury and Chas Jankel (Blackhill Music); 'American Pie' (p. 125) written Don McLean (United Artists Music); 'It Will Stand' (p. 126) written Norman Johnson (Commodore Imperial).

Other sources   The Elvis Presley quote in the epigraph is from Mick Farren (ed.), *Elvis In His Own Words* (Omnibus Press, 1977); the quote at the top of p. 3 is from *Rock'n'Roll News*, no. 10; Tennessee Teddy (p. 3) is from *Rock'n'Roll Collector*, no. 4; the quote on pp. 5–6 is from Stanley Booth, 'A Hound Dog To The Manor Born' in J. Eisen (ed.), *The Age Of Rock* (Random House, 1969); the first quote on p. 6 is from Jeff Nuttall, *Bomb Culture* (Paladin, 1970); the second quote on p. 6 is from *Daily Sketch*, 14 September 1956; Bill Haley (p. 14) from *New Kommotion*, no. 15, Spring 1977; the quotes on pp. 18–19 respectively from *Melody Maker*, 5 May 1956, *New Musical Express*, 4 January 1957, and *Daily Sketch*, 4 September 1956; Nik Cohn (pp. 19 and 112) are from N. Cohn, *AWopBopALooBopALopBamBoom* (Paladin, 1970); George Hay (p. 23) from Bill C. Malone, *Country Music USA* (University of Texas Press, 1968); the quote on pp. 23–24 from Dave Johnson in *Country Music Review*, October 1977; Bill Monroe (p. 24) from *Old Time Music*, no. 16, Spring 1975; Wesley Rose (p. 27) from Roger M. Williams, *Sing A Sad Song – The Life Of Hank Williams* (Ballantine Books, 1973); Hank Williams (p. 27) from Ralph J. Gleason, 'Hank Williams, Roy Acuff And Then God!!' in *Rolling Stone*, 28 June 1969; Carl Perkins (pp. 49, 50, and 94) and Jerry Lee Lewis (p. 53) are from Michael Lydon, *Rock Folk* (Dell, 1971); Buddy Holly (p. 29) and Scotty Moore (p. 30) from John J. Goldrosen, *Buddy Holly – His Life And Music* (Charisma Books, 1975); Johnny Otis (p. 31) from Rolling Stone Editors, *The Rolling Stone Interviews Volume 2* (Straight Arrow, 1973); Alan Freed (p. 35) from *Rock'n'Roll News*, no. 4; Sam Phillips (pp. 35, 36 and 40), Marion Keisker (pp. 37 and 38), Buzzie Forbess (pp. 39 and 40), Scotty Moore (p. 39), Bob Neal (p. 41) and the quotes on pp. 45 and 48 from Jerry Hopkins, *Elvis* (Sphere Books, 1974); Greil Marcus (p. 38) and the quote on p. 48 from Greil Marcus, *Mystery Train* (E. P. Dutton, 1975); Bob Luman (p. 42) from Paul Hemphill, *The Nashville Sound – Bright Lights And Country Music* (Simon & Schuster, 1970); Ronnie Hawkins (p. 50), Jerry Lee Lewis (p. 51), Elvis Presley (p. 103) and Johnny Thunders (p. 133) are included in Jonathon Green, the *Book Of Rock Quotes* (Omnibus Press, 1977); the quotes on pp. 54, 118 and 120 from Rob Finnis and Bob Dunham, *Gene Vincent and The Blue Caps* (c. the authors, 1974); the first quote on p. 61 from Langdon Winner in Jim Miller (ed.), *The Rolling Stone Illustrated History Of Rock And Roll* (Rolling Stone Press, Random House, 1976); the second quote and Fats Domino (p. 56) and the quote on p. 62 from newsreel footage included in the film *Let The Good Times Roll* (Columbia Pictures, 1973); Peter Guralnick (p. 61), from P. Guralnick, *Feel Like Goin' Home* (Omnibus Press,

1978); John Lennon (p. 71) from Hunter Davies, *The Beatles* (Heinemann, 1968); the quote on p. 72 from *Daily Sketch*, 18 September 1956; the quotes on p. 75 from *Melody Maker*, January 1978; Jet Harris (p. 78) from Royston Ellis (ed.), *The Shadows By Themselves* (Souvenir Press, 1961); Tommy Steele (pp. 78 and 83) from Michael Gray in *Let It Rock*, no. 27, March 1975; John Kennedy (pp. 78–80) from J. Kennedy, *Tommy Steele* (Souvenir Press, 1958); Terry Dene (p. 81) and Pete Murray (p. 107) are from *Melody Maker*, 17 February 1968; the other quotes on pp. 81–3 from Dan Wooding, *I Thought Terry Dene Was Dead* (Coverdale House, 1974); Lenny Kaye quotes Jerry Capehart (p. 89) in his sleevenotes to 'Legendary Masters – Eddie Cochran' (United Artists, UAD 60017/8); Ricky Nelson (p. 91) from Colin Escott and Martin Hawkins, *Catalyst: The Sun Records Story* (Aquarius Books, 1975); Bill Haley (p. 94) from 'Rock'n'Roll Personality Parade' from *New Musical Express*, 1957; Ian Sippen quotes Link Wray (p. 100) in his sleevenotes to Link Wray, *'There's Good Rockin' Tonite'* (Union Pacific, UP 002); Dick Clark (p. 103) from *The Book of Rock Quotes* (Omnibus Press, 1977); Fabian (p. 104) from Pete Bryant in *SMG*, no. 12, April/May 1974; the quote on p. 105 from Langdon Winner in Greil Marcus (ed.), *Rock And Roll Will Stand* (Beacon Press, 1969); Pete Murray (p. 108) from *New Musical Express*, 28 February 1958); Jack Good (pp. 108–9) from Royston Ellis, *The Big Beat Scene* (Four Square Books, 1961); Marty Wilde (p. 110) from *New Musical Express*, 11 September 1959; the quotes on p. 117, from *New Musical Express*, 27 June 1958 and John Grissim in *Rolling Stone*, 17 September 1970, respectively; Johnny Kidd (p. 122) from *New Musical Express*, 12 August 1960; the quote at the top of p. 127 from *Stevenson's Book of Quotations* (Cassell, 6th edn, 1946, p. 2298; attributed to Victor Hugo); Ray Gosling (p. 127) from a BBC radio programme, and Harold Macmillan (p. 128) from a speech at Bedford on 20 July 1957: both are quoted in Theo Barker (ed.), *The Long March Of Everyman 1750–1960* (Penguin, 1978); Rockin' Robin (p. 132) is from *Rock'n'Roll News*, no. 10; Alan Freed is quoted by John Morthland in Jim Miller (ed.), *The Rolling Stone Illustrated History Of Rock And Roll* (Rolling Stone Press, Random House, 1976).

Pictures   pp. 26, 32, 34, 51, 52, 55, 57, 59, 62, 65, 67, 100, Bill Greensmith; pp. 47, 68, 87, 90, 93, 113, 114, 115, John Beecher; pp. 4, 5, 14, 20, 76, 79, 80, the Radio Times Hulton Picture Library; pp. 9, 10, 85, the National Film Archive Stills Library; pp. 82, 110, the Camera Press; p. 19, Roger Mayne. Author and publishers are grateful to the above for permission to reproduce copyright material.

Special thanks to my friend Dave Stephens for his invaluable help in providing information and answering all sorts of questions; and to Anne and David Scott, in whose house much of this book was written.

Some suggestions for further reading and listening

Books   The most complete history of rock'n'roll is
Charlie Gillett, *The Sound Of The City* (Sphere Books, 1971).
But see also the relevant articles (and pictures) in
Jim Miller (ed.), *The Rolling Stone Illustrated History Of Rock'n'Roll* (Rolling Stone Press, Random House, 1976).
And, for a highly entertaining, personal view, the early chapters of
Nik Cohn, *AWopBopaLooBopaLopBamBoom* (Paladin, 1970).
For the story of Sam Phillips and Sun Records see
Colin Escott and Martin Hawkins, *Catalyst – The Sun Records Story* (Aquarius Books, 1975).
The following are also well worth reading – they do much more than just tell the stories of the artists concerned:
John Goldrosen, *Buddy Holly, His Life And Music* (Charisma Books 1975).
Jerry Hopkins, *Elvis* (Sphere Books, 1974).
However, the best writing on Elvis is in Greil Marcus:
Mystery Train (Omnibus Press, 1977), whose main theme is 'to deal with rock'n'roll not as youth culture, or counter culture, but simply as American culture'.
There are few books on rock'n'roll's impact on Britain, but the following are a good start:
John Kennedy, *Tommy Steele* (Souvenir Press, 1958). Long out of print but a library should easily provide a copy.
Chris May, *Rock'n'Roll* (Sociopack Publications Ltd, 1974) – includes an illustrated section on Jack Good's *Oh Boy!*
The following are recommended for social, political and

historical background on the 1950s:

Peter Lewis, *The Fifties* (Heinemann, 1978)

Colin MacInnes, *Absolute Beginners* (MacGibbon & Kee, 1959/Panther, 1972). An entertaining and perceptive novel about a late-1950s London teenager.

Alan Thompson, *The Day Before Yesterday* (Panther/ Sidgwick & Jackson, 1971)

Recordings   Hank Williams, *40 Greatest Hits* (Polydor MGM 2683 071) contains his most well-known songs.

City rhythm'n'blues, from bands to vocal groups, is well represented on *The Roots Of Rock'n'Roll* (Savoy SJL 2221).

Some of the best black music Sam Phillips recorded in the early 1950s is on *The Blues Came Down From Memphis* (Charly CR 30125).

Bill Haley and his Comets: *Rock Around The Clock* (MCA CDL 8017).

Elvis at Sun Records before signing with RCA is on –

Elvis Presley, *The Sun Collection* (RCA Starcall HY 1001).

The following compilations are the cheapest, the most representative, or the most accessible – but not always all three:

Carl Perkins, *The Original Carl Perkins* (Charly CR 30110).

Jerry Lee Lewis, *The Original Jerry Lee Lewis* (Charly CR 30111).

Gene Vincent, *Greatest* (Capitol CAPS 1001).

Fats Domino, *20 Greatest Hits* (United Artists UAS 29967).

Chuck Berry, *Motorvatin'* (Chess 9286 690).

Little Richard, *20 Original Hits* (Sonet SNTF 5017).

Buddy Holly and the Crickets, *20 Golden Greats* (MCA EMTV 8).

Eddie Cochran, *15th Anniversary Album* (United Artists UAG 29760).

Some of the best doo-wop singles (as well as the voice of Alan Freed!) can be heard on *Alan Freed's Memory Lane* (Pye PKL 5572).

And in Britain:

Lonnie Donegan: *The Donegan File* (Pye FILD 011)

Cliff Richard's early rock'n'roll releases – 'Move It', 'High Class Baby', 'Livin' Lovin' Doll' and 'Mean Streak' – are now available again as singles.

Billy Fury, *The Billy Fury Story* (Decca DPA 3033/4).

Johnny Kidd and the Pirates, *The Best of Johnny Kidd and the Pirates* (EMI NUTM 12).
Finally, excerpts from the TV show *Oh Boy!* can be found on:
Various, *Jack Good's 'Oh Boy!'* (EMI NUTM 13).

Index